CIAO y'all

RECIPES FROM THE PBS SERIES CUCINA AMORE

Bright Sky Press

Box 416, Albany, Texas 76430

Photographs by:
Diane Padys, L'Image Magick, Inc. and Watt M. Casey, Jr.
Text by:
John DeMers
Book Design by:
Tina Taylor
Edited by:
Sunday Kornye
Printed in China through Asia Pacific Offset

10 9 8 7 6 5 4 3 2

Library of Congress Cataloging-in-Publication Data

Mandola, Damian, 1952-
Ciao y'all / Damian Mandola & Johnny Carrabba;
forword by Chris T. Sullivan;
photography by Diane Padys and Watt Casey, Jr.
p. cm.
ISBN 1-931721-19-X (cloth : alk. Paper)
1. Cookery, Italian.   2. Cucina amore (Television program)
I. Carrabba, Johnny, 1958-   II. Title.

TX723.M317 2002
641.5945--dc21   2002028378

Cucina Amore is produced by West 175 Productions, Inc.
in association with Thirteen/WNET New York

West 175 Productions
1959 NW Dock Place, Suite 3
Seattle, WA 98107
www.cucinaamore.com

Funding for *Cucina Amore* is provided by:

CIAO y'all

RECIPES FROM THE PBS SERIES CUCINA AMORE

**Damian Mandola &
Johnny Carrabba**

FOREWORD BY CHRIS T. SULLIVAN

PHOTOGRAPHY BY DIANE PADYS
& WATT M. CASEY, JR.

Text by John DeMers

Table of Contents

DEDICATION

To my Mamma, Grace, the greatest cook I ever knew, who not only taught me the basics of good cooking but also the importance of having family gather at the table, often. —Damian Mandola

To all the women in my life, who have the toughest responsibility: raising a family. Maw Maw Carrabba Vento, Maw Maw Mandola, my loving mother Rose, my beautiful wife Brandy and my baby daughter Mia Rose. Thank you for setting the pace for our family! —Johnny Carrabba

Left to right: Vincent Mandola (Damian's brother) atop Texas, Aunt Margaret Mandola Lampasas, Aunt Phil Dorsa and Mamma Grace Mandola, at the Texas-Oklahoma border.

Foreword

A PARTNERSHIP BUILT ON PASSION

I first visited Johnny Carrabba and Damian Mandola in 1993 at the urging of one of my business partners.

Arriving at one of their family-owned restaurants in Houston, I was immediately struck by their warm embraces, hearty laughter and lively conversation—not just to me—but towards every guest who walked through the door.

I was hooked. At Carrabba's, I found the Italian gusto for food, family and life deep in the heart of Texas.

This, I thought, is what passion is all about. I saw it in Johnny's eyes, words and actions. I tasted it in Damian's gifts with food and wine. And, I observed it as guest after guest dined, enthralled with the authentic aromas, flavors and generous spirit that emanated from every corner of the room, and from every member of the staff.

It is a passion, I discovered, that the entire family possessed: from Johnny's mom and dad, Rose and John Jr., Damian's mom and Johnny's grandmother Grace, to Johnny and Damian themselves. The Carrabbas' and Mandolas' passion was contagious—and I wanted us to be a part of it.

That initial evening eventually led to a partnership that, to this day, continues to generate positive outcomes. I am deeply grateful to the Carrabba and Mandola families. The passion they instilled in us has allowed us to share the genuine hospitality of their Italian family, and their extraordinary recipes with guests all over the country.

It has truly been a wonderful ten years with Carrabba's Italian Grill.

Thank you, Johnny, Damian, Rose, John Jr., Grace and all of the Carrabba and Mandola families. You are all magnifico!

—Chris T. Sullivan
Founder & CEO of Outback Steakhouse, Inc.

Introduction

We're not real chefs. We're real eaters. We don't mean diners, gourmands or bon vivants. We're two big Sicilian boys from Texas who love to cook and eat. We love the Sicilian food our parents and grandparents cooked. We love the Creole and Southern food our family members picked up passing through Louisiana and stepping off the boat right on the dock in Galveston. And we love the Western food that's just part of being in Texas.

Food, you see, isn't only about food. It's not some big secret. It's something that just happens when all of our interconnected families get together—the Carrabbas and the Mandolas, plus anybody with enough good sense to marry in. You may be poor, went the saying a mere generation ago, but you'll never be hungry. Food was and still is part of everything we do, and not just because we run our own restaurants. Food is part of us because that's how we were raised; food was present at births, christenings, weddings, graduations and funerals.

Food is what reminded us we were family. To this day, whenever one family member meets another and starts talking about something or someplace, the first question has to be, "Whadya eat?"

Our Texas accents may be strange to you, especially when you're watching a PBS cooking series with a name like *Cucina Amore*. Let's just say, we don't find our accents strange at all. We talk the way we grew up talking along the Gulf Coast, just like we cook and eat the way we grew up cooking and eating.

Damian at his resteraunt, D'Amico's, 1978.

Our Gulf Coast experience is about the place where all of our ancestors came to build their lives. They called it America! And they didn't just mean Ellis Island, or Little Italy in New York, or the North End of Boston or South Philly. They meant the whole damn place, wherever it began and ended, which of course nobody much knew. And it meant an idea too, a big promise in the air during the hard times in Sicily that if you sacrificed just about everything and pretty near worked yourself to death, you could have something a little better. Which, after all, was exactly what you did in the Old Country—without any promise at all.

So they came, ship after ship full of them. Full of us. And all the while, there were other ships filled with other people, speaking different languages. In America, we would come to know them all. And talk with them all. And wrestle with them all. And, in some cases, cook with them all. We kept on being who we are, sure enough, but after a while we were something different, too. Something entirely new.

So give us a break here. Don't go picking over our grandma's and mamma's and aunt's and uncle's recipes, whining about this not being the way they did it at your house. Great! We'll go to your house and eat again later. Right now, you're at our house. And at our house, this is the way the old folks taught the young folks. This is the way we remember things tasting. And this is what it all comes down to—with generous sprinklings of life, love and oregano—for two big Sicilian boys from Texas who love to cook and eat.

—Damian Mandola and Johnny Carrabba

Appetizers

Antipasti

From the time the first Sicilians landed along the Gulf Coast of Texas and Louisiana, they lived to eat and ate to live. Times were hard here though not as hard as back home in Sicilia. So each meal blended a lot of survival with at least a little celebration.

We don't know about you, but we love appetizers. It's not that they're easier to cook than entrées—sometimes they can be pretty difficult. It's just that growing up in the Mandola and Carrabba families taught us to taste everything that ever went by on a plate. In fact, the more different kinds of food, the better. So that's why we love appetizers so much. Apps are just more fun, we think. They give off a warm welcome (yes, even when they're cold), along with an effort to break the ice and make everybody feel comfortable. These pictures are from our family album. One shows Johnny's great-great grandma Nita Palazzo, along with his great aunt Nita Palazzo Carrabba (the little girl). The other photo is of Mamma Grace Mandola, the "Mamma" of many of our recipes.

Nita Palazzo Carrabba with Great-Great Grandmother Nita Palazzo

Grace Mandola

Eggplant Relish

Eggplant Relish
Caponata

SERVES 6–8

- 1/2 cup olive oil
- 1 medium eggplant, skin left on, cut into 1/2-inch (1.5 cm) dice
- 2 cups celery, cut into 1/4-inch (6 mm) dice
- 1 large onion, cut into 1/4-inch (6 mm) dice
- 2 tablespoons tomato paste
- 2 large tomatoes, peeled, seeded and diced (see page 181)
- 1/3 cup red wine vinegar
- 1 1/2 teaspoons sugar
- 1 cup water
- Kosher salt and freshly-ground black pepper
- 1/4 cup pitted Calamata olives, cut in half
- 1/4 cup pitted green olives, cut in half
- 1 tablespoon capers
- 2 tablespoons pine nuts, toasted (see page 180)
- 1 cup chopped fresh Italian parsley
- 2 tablespoons chopped fresh oregano

TO PREPARE

1 In a large sauté pan, heat the olive oil on high until it sizzles, about three minutes. Reduce the heat to medium, add the eggplant and leave on one side to cook for four minutes. Then stir the eggplant around and cook another four minutes until it's very tender. Remove the eggplant from the pan, saving the oil, and set aside.

2 Add the celery and onion to the same pan and add a little more oil if necessary. Sauté the onion and celery until tender, about five minutes. Return the eggplant to the pan with the celery and onion.

3 Add the tomato paste, tomatoes, vinegar, sugar, water and salt and pepper to taste. Cook over medium heat for another five minutes. Remove from the heat and add the Calamata and green olives, capers, pine nuts, parsley and oregano. Transfer to a bowl and refrigerate overnight.

To serve

Bring the caponata to room temperature. Serve on or with slices of toasted rustic bread, or on the side with crackers.

This is something we always had around. I remember getting home from football practice when I was a kid and fixing myself a *caponata* sandwich. –Johnny

That's Sicilian—except for the football practice. –Damian

13

Wild Mushroom Tart
Crostata di Funghi

SERVES 6–8. MAKES ONE 11-INCH (28 CM) TART

1	recipe Cornmeal Tart Dough (see page 168 for recipe)
2	tablespoons olive oil
2	cups wild mushrooms, such as hedgehog and chanterelles, sliced 1/4-inch thick
2	cups crimini mushrooms, sliced
	Kosher salt and freshly-ground black pepper
1	onion or 4 large shallots, sliced 1/2-inch (1.5 cm) thick and caramelized (see page 182)
1/2	cup dried porcini or morel mushrooms, reconstituted in 1 cup hot water for 30 minutes, drained with the liquid reserved separately, and minced
1	tablespoon chopped fresh Italian parsley
1/2	teaspoon chopped fresh thyme
1/2	teaspoon chopped fresh oregano
1/2	teaspoon chopped fresh rosemary
5	eggs
3/4	cup grated Parmigiano Reggiano cheese
1	cup heavy cream

TO PREPARE THE DOUGH

On a lightly-floured board, roll out the dough to about 1/4-inch (6 mm) thick. Line an 11 x 1-inch (28 x 2.5 cm) fluted tart pan, or a glass or porcelain baking dish, with the dough and set aside. Preheat the oven to 350° F (180° C).

TO PREPARE THE FILLING

1 Heat the olive oil on medium high in a large sauté pan until it sizzles, about two minutes.
2 Add the wild mushrooms, crimini mushrooms and salt and pepper to taste and cook for two minutes to sweat the juices out.
3 Add the caramelized onions or shallots and the drained porcini and cook for 1 1/2 minutes. Add the white wine and reserved porcini liquid and cook for 1 1/2 minutes to reduce the liquid.
4 Transfer to a bowl, stir in the herbs and cool for about 10 minutes.
5 In a mixing bowl, beat the eggs and a pinch of salt and pepper. Add the Parmigiano Reggiano cheese and heavy cream and mix well. Add the cooled mushroom mixture.

6 Pour into the dough-lined tart pan and bake for about 45 minutes until it sets up. (Quickly put a sharp knife or toothpick in the center of it, if it comes out clean the tart is "setup".) Let the tart cool for 10 minutes, or more, before slicing. Serve hot or room temperature.

To serve

Garnish the top of each piece with Italian parsley and serve.

I make this a lot, especially when I can make it ahead for company. You can serve it warm or at room temperature. It's a low-maintenance-type recipe. –Johnny

If you're being fussy, you can make your own crust. But it's real good on frozen crust, too. –Damian

Sun-Dried Tomato-Pâté Canapés

Crostini di Pomodori Secchi

SERVES 4–6

3	tablespoons extra-virgin olive oil
3	cloves garlic, peeled and minced
3	anchovy fillets, minced
3	tablespoons capers
1/4	cup white wine
2	cups peeled, seeded and roughly-chopped tomatoes (see page 181)
1/2	cup oil-packed sun-dried tomatoes, finely chopped
3	tablespoons chopped fresh Italian parsley
	Kosher salt and freshly-ground black pepper
1	recipe Bruschetta (see page 176)

TO PREPARE

1 To make the tomato pâté, heat the olive oil in a sauté pan on medium-high heat. Add the garlic cloves, anchovy fillets, and capers and sauté for about two minutes until the garlic starts to turn a light brown.

2 Pour in the wine, chopped tomatoes and sun-dried tomatoes. Simmer until the liquid is reduced, about one minute, and the mixture has a spread-able consistency.

3 Remove from the stove, put the ingredients into a food processor and pulse quickly. Transfer to a bowl and stir in the Italian parsley. Season with salt and pepper to taste. Set aside.

4 Prepare the Bruschetta.

To serve

Arrange the bruschetta on a large plate with the tomato pâté either on the side or spread on the bruschetta.

Bruschetta? That's pretty much Italian toast, isn't it, Big D? —Johnny

Well, once you brush it with enough olive oil and garlic and then spread it with this tomato pâté, boy, toast never had it so good. —Damian

It's really easy, too! —Johnny

Tomatoes Sicilian-Style
Pomodori Siciliani

SERVES 4–6

4	large ripe tomatoes, cored and cut into 6 wedges
1	small red onion, sliced thin, soaked in cold water for 30 minutes, and drained
8	pitted black olives, roughly chopped
1/2	cup grated Ricotta Salata (see page 176)
1	tablespoon chopped fresh oregano or 1/4 teaspoon dried
1/4	cup white or red wine vinegar
1/2	cup extra-virgin olive oil
	Kosher salt and freshly-ground black pepper
1	recipe Bruschetta (see page 176)
4	whole basil leaves, torn into thirds, for garnish

TO PREPARE

1 In a large bowl, toss together the tomatoes, onion, olives, 1/4 cup Ricotta Salata, oregano, vinegar, a little olive oil and salt and pepper to taste. Set aside.

2 Prepare the Bruschetta.

To serve

Lay the bruschetta on a large plate. Arrange the tomato mixture over the top of the bruschetta. Make sure you use some of that good juice that is on the bottom of the bowl. Garnish with the remaining Ricotta Salata and the torn basil leaves. This dish can also be served as a salad with some good crusty rustic bread to sop up that juice.

Mamma Mandola, Damian's mom, or as we call her, "Amazing Grace", was really good with tomatoes. She made this recipe all the time. She never overdid it with the oregano, always somehow using just enough. –Johnny

This is one of those Sicilian-tasting dishes. It's very earthy and very good. –Damian

Left to right: Frances Ditta, Lena Vallone, Aunt Frances Mandola Corona, Mamma Grace Mandola and Mary Margaret Corona at a wedding reception in the early 60's.

Stuffed Tomatoes with Tuna

Pomodori Ripieni con Tonno

SERVES 6

MAYONNAISE INGREDIENTS

2	egg yolks
1	clove garlic, peeled, crushed and minced
1	teaspoon Dijon mustard
	Juice of half a lemon
	Kosher salt and freshly-ground black pepper
1/2	cup extra-virgin olive oil
1/2	cup vegetable oil

TOMATO AND TUNA INGREDIENTS

6	fresh Roma tomatoes, blanched and peeled (see page 181)
1	5-ounce (150 g) can tuna packed in water, drained and broken up into chunks
1	tablespoon capers, finely chopped
1	tablespoon chopped fresh Italian parsley
2	tablespoons extra-virgin olive oil
	Kosher salt and freshly-ground black pepper

TO PREPARE THE MAYONNAISE

1 Put the egg yolks, garlic, Dijon mustard, lemon juice and a pinch of salt and pepper into a medium-sized mixing bowl.

2 Using a whisk, drizzle in the olive oil and the vegetable oil while mixing. Make sure each drop of oil is mixed in thoroughly before adding the next. After you've added several drops of oil, the mixture will begin to thicken. At that stage you can begin to add the oil in larger drops. Beat vigorously until all the oil is used. Taste and season again. Add a little bit of lemon juice if the consistency needs thinning. Set aside.

If you've ever spent time along the Gulf in the summer, you'll know why we like cold dishes just like this. It's so light. –Damian

That's why I serve this with macaroni and cheese. –Johnny

Yeah, I serve mine with chicken fried steak. –Damian

TO STUFF THE TOMATOES

1 Cut the tomatoes in half lengthwise and remove the seeds and pulp. Line the tomatoes open-side-up on a serving platter and set aside.

2 In another mixing bowl, mix together the tuna, capers, parsley, extra-virgin olive oil and about 1/4 to 1/3 cup of the mayonnaise, just enough so that it's moist but not too soupy. Season with salt and pepper to taste.

To serve

Fill the tomato halves with the tuna mixture, garnish each with a dollop of mayonnaise on top and serve.

NOTE: Any leftover mayonnaise should be stored in a screw-top glass jar in the bottom of your refrigerator for no longer than one week.

Cannellini Bean Purée with Bruschetta

Cannellini Bean Purée with Grilled Bread
Crostini con Purea di Fagioli

SERVES 4–6

PURÉE INGREDIENTS

Cannellini beans, boiled (see below) or 2 15-ounce (440 g) cans cannellini or white kidney beans, drained, water reserved

1/2 cup roasted garlic cloves (see page 180)

1/2 cup extra-virgin olive oil

1 tablespoon chopped fresh rosemary

Kosher salt and freshly-ground black pepper

1 roasted red bell pepper for garnish (see page 181)

1 recipe Bruschetta (see page 176)

BOILED CANNELLINI INGREDIENTS

3/4 pound (340 g) dried cannellini beans, soaked overnight

5 quarts (4.75 l) water

1 teaspoon kosher salt

1 tablespoon olive oil

2 fresh sage leaves

TO PREPARE

1 Rinse beans and place in a large pot. Add remaining ingredients. Place pot on a medium-high flame and bring to a boil. Reduce heat and simmer two or three hours or until the beans are tender.

2 Remove pot from stove and let beans cool completely in the water they were boiled in. Drain beans, reserving the bean boiling water. Remove sage leaves. Proceed with the recipe.

TO PREPARE THE PURÉE

1 To make the purée place the beans, roasted garlic and rosemary in a food processor. Turn the machine on and drizzle in the extra-virgin olive oil until the purée has a spreadable consistency. Add more oil if needed, or substitute a little reserved bean water if you don't want to use any more oil. Season with the salt and pepper to taste. Set aside.

2 Prepare the Bruschetta.

To serve

Spread the bean purée on the bruschetta, then lay a few strips of roasted red pepper on top of each one and arrange on a large plate. You can also serve the purée on the side in a large bowl and garnish by chopping the roasted red pepper and sprinkling it on top.

APPETIZERS

19

Marinated Olives
Olive Scacciate

MAKES ONE GALLON

2   pounds (900 g) green olives, lightly crushed to break the skin
2   pounds (900 g) Calamata olives, pitted and crushed
2¹/₂ cups peeled and medium-diced carrots
3   cups medium-diced celery
¹/₂   cup coarsely-chopped garlic
¹/₂   cup chopped fresh basil
¹/₄   cup chopped fresh mint
2   tablespoons chopped fresh oregano
2   tablespoons freshly-ground black pepper
2   cups extra-virgin olive oil + 2 cups extra to cover the top
1¹/₂ cups red wine vinegar

TO PREPARE

Place all the ingredients in a large 1-gallon (3.75 l) jar. Shake the jar to ensure all the spices, vinegar and oil are well blended. Top off the jar with extra-virgin olive oil and cover.

To serve

Remove from the jar and drain the olive oil. This is great served as a side with any of our great bruschetta recipes or as part of an antipasto.

In Sicily, *scacciate* means "to crush." –Damian

So this means "crushed or cracked" olives? –Johnny

That's right! Which is what we do before we marinate them. –Damian

Boy, I remember Papa, Damian's dad. He'd always buy hard salami, mozzarella, you know, everything on butcher paper, and we'd eat right off it. And he'd always have some olives, just like this. –Johnny

This recipe is great because the olives keep indefinitely in the refrigerator as long as they are covered by the oil. –Damian

Garlic Olive-Oil Dip
Bagna Caôda

SERVES 4–6

DIP INGREDIENTS

5–6	cloves garlic, peeled and chopped fine
1	cup extra-virgin olive oil
2	ounces (60 g) anchovy fillets, finely chopped
1/2	cup butter
1	teaspoon grated fresh lemon zest
1	small dried red chili pepper

VEGETABLE INGREDIENTS

4	fresh baby artichokes, trimmed, cut in half lengthwise and blanched for 10 minutes (see page 181)
1	large fennel bulb with leaves trimmed off and outer ribs removed, cut into 8 pieces
1	head radicchio or Belgian endive, (use individual leaves for serving)
1	zucchini, sliced into 1/2-inch (1.5 cm) thick rounds
1/2	red bell pepper, cut into 1-inch (2.5 cm) wide strips
1/2	yellow bell pepper, cut into 1-inch (2.5 cm) wide strips

ADDITIONAL INGREDIENTS

12	slices rustic bread

TO PREPARE

This recipe requires a fondue pot.

1 Place garlic and olive oil in a medium saucepan over low heat. Simmer for five to eight minutes, until the garlic starts to soften, do not let garlic brown. Stir in the anchovies and simmer a few minutes until the anchovies dissolve.

2 Add the butter, lemon zest and chili pepper.

3 Simmer for three to four minutes and set aside.

To serve

Arrange the vegetables on a large platter with the bread slices. Reheat the dip and pour into a fondue pot with a votive underneath to keep warm. Dunk the vegetables in the dip and use bread slices to catch any drippings.

In the Piedmont of Italy, *bagna caôda* means "hot bath." —Damian

It's about how these vegetables get "bathed" in the olive oil anchovy and garlic. —Johnny

Over there they use olive oil and anchovies the way we pour on Ranch dressing in Texas. —Damian

Mussels and Clams with Pancetta
Cozze e Vongole con Pancetta

SERVES 4–6

1	pound (450 g) little neck clams, cleaned (see page 182)
1	pound (450 g) mussels, cleaned (see page 182)
2	tablespoons olive oil
2	cups pancetta, diced
2	cloves garlic, peeled and minced
1	tablespoon whole fennel seeds, toasted in a dry sauté pan over medium heat until fragrant
1	tablespoon crushed chilies
1	cup white wine
1	lemon
2	tablespoons butter
	Kosher salt and freshly-ground black pepper
1	sprig Italian parsley, chopped

TO PREPARE

1 Wash the clams in cold running water with a little salt to help purge them of sand and grit. Clean the mussels under cold water as well, and pull off the beards prior to cooking, using a towel to help grip the beard itself.

2 In a large skillet, heat the olive oil over medium-high heat until sizzling, about two minutes. Brown the pancetta, about four to five minutes and add the garlic, fennel and crushed chilies.

3 Stir and cook two more minutes and then place the clams and mussels in the pan. Cook for one minute, then deglaze with the wine. Cover and cook for three to five minutes, until the clams and mussels have opened.

4 Remove the lid, squeeze in the lemon and add the butter, and salt and pepper to taste.

To serve

Garnish with chopped parsley and serve right from the pot, in a large bowl, or in individual bowls. Great served with country Italian bread to dip in the broth.

Just about any time you steam something with a little tomato and olive oil, it becomes Mediterranean. –Damian

And then there's the pancetta, Italian bacon. –Johnny

This is one of the dishes we serve that people love the most. –Damian

Not everybody eats mussels. But the folks who love mussels *really* love ours. –Johnny

You can also use all clams or all mussels in this recipe, if you prefer. –Damian

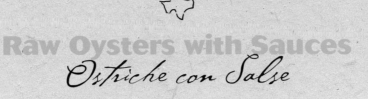

SERVES 2

1 dozen fresh, raw oysters, scrubbed under cold running
water and chilled well for easier shucking (see page 182)

Crushed Ice

OPTIONAL CONDIMENTS

Mignonette Sauce (see page 173)

Cocktail Sauce (see page 172)

Lemon wedges

TO PREPARE

1 To shuck an oyster: With one hand in a heavy oven mitt, hold the oyster, flat side up, firmly against a cutting board.

2 Using a strong-bladed oyster knife with a hand guard, insert the knife tip between the shells near the hinge, being careful that the knife blade doesn't slip.

3 Twist the blade and push it into the opening, prying the oyster open. Move the blade along the inside of the upper shell to free the muscle from the shell.

4 Remove and discard the top shell of the oyster. Slide the knife under the oyster to sever the muscle from the bottom shell.

To serve

Make sure the oysters are neatly nestled in their half shells and discard any loose bits of shell that might be floating around. Arrange them on a large plate or tray of crushed ice and serve with one or all of the optional condiments.

Okay, so we don't make the raw oysters. But we sure do know how to eat them.

–Johnny

Growing up on the Gulf Coast, we'd always go out to my aunt's in Kemah. The whole family would be there. We'd just sit around in a circle and a couple of the uncles would start shucking. –Damian

We'd get the oysters in big burlap bags. We called them croaker sacks. –Johnny

When you picture a bunch of uncles, fathers and grandfathers shucking all these great Gulf oysters, you know oysters go back a long way with us. –Damian

Grandpa Joe Testa's store in Sunrise, Louisiana

Salads & Soups
Insalate e Zuppe

Salads always provided a nice cooling touch, especially during those hot Texas summers. But around our family, soups were some of the best things going. We had a lot of meals with soups as the main course. In fact, if you put enough meat in it and salad all around it, it can still be a pretty substantial meal.

If you find a meatless soup you like, you'll know it was developed for Friday supper, back in the days when Catholics ate no meat on Friday. If you find a favorite with meat in it, it almost certainly turned up on Monday evening—it really hit the spot after the huge family feast of Sunday.

These photos are scenes from the early life of Sicilians in Louisiana and Texas—from the life of a grandfather named Joe Testa, to be precise. One shows the grocery store he started in Sunrise, La., when he and Grandma were newlyweds from Cefalú in Sicily. The other photo shows the making of what might have been the family fortune. Grandpa made a soft drink named Testa-Cola. All of us in the family think it's a shame that the other cola caught on instead.

Grandpa Joe Testa,
(center, facing camera) in Testa-Cola
Bottling Plant in Alexandria, Lousianna

Blood Orange and Dandelion Salad
Insalata di Taroco e Cicoria

SERVES 4–6

VINAIGRETTE INGREDIENTS

2   shallots, minced

$1/2$ cup sherry vinegar

      Juice of one blood orange

      Kosher salt and freshly-ground black pepper

$1 1/2$ cups extra-virgin olive oil

SALAD INGREDIENTS

$1 1/2$ pounds (750 g) dandelion greens, cleaned
      (can substitute baby spinach or arugula)

5   blood oranges, peeled and sliced crosswise
      into $1/2$-inch (1.5 cm) thick rounds

$1/2$ cup Pecorino Romano cheese, shaved

TO PREPARE

1 In a mixing bowl, whisk together the shallots, sherry vinegar, blood orange juice and salt and pepper to taste. Slowly whisk in the olive oil until fully incorporated.

2 Add the greens to the bowl and toss well with the vinaigrette to coat evenly.

To serve

Place the greens in the middle of a large platter or on individual serving plates. Arrange the orange slices around the outside of the greens and top with the shaved Pecorino Romano cheese.

I remember the first time I ever tasted blood oranges. I was in Sicily with Damian at the time. Growing up, we ate orange salads often but we always used regular oranges. Using blood oranges just makes it better. –Johnny

Both my grandpa and my dad made a salad similar to this, using sweet oranges. I thought it was so unusual. In Sicily, it was nice to discover that everybody over there ate it too. –Damian

Italian Potato Salad
Insalata di Patate

SERVES 4–6

DRESSING INGREDIENTS

3	tablespoons roasted garlic purée (see page 180)
1/4	cup red wine vinegar
1/8	cup sherry vinegar
1	cup extra-virgin olive oil

SALAD INGREDIENTS

3	pounds (1.4 kg) Yellow Finn potatoes
1	red onion, peeled and cut into medium dice
1	bunch green onion, peeled and sliced
1	cup celery hearts, coarsely chopped
3/4	cup oil-cured olives, pitted and chopped
1	tablespoon fennel seed, toasted
	Kosher salt and freshly-ground black pepper
1/2	bunch Italian parsley, whole leaves

TO PREPARE

1 Bring to a boil enough water to cover the potatoes. Salt the boiling water then add the potatoes. Boil them until a knife can be easily inserted in the middle of a few to test if cooked. When cooked, drain the potatoes and cut them into quarters and put them into a large mixing bowl with the remaining salad ingredients.

2 For the dressing, crush the roasted garlic with a spoon. Using a whisk, stir in the vinegars and slowly add the olive oil until it's all incorporated. Pour the dressing over the salad ingredients and toss well.

To serve

Put the salad on a platter and drizzle more extra-virgin olive oil over the top.

This is not your typical mayonnaise-y potato salad. It's real clean, with olives and olive oil plus the crunch of celery. –Damian

Growin' up, this would be summertime food to go along with the barbecue. My Aunt Frances and Uncle Charlie Corona had a beach house in Seabrook, Texas. That's where we ate potato salad the most. –Johnny

Left to right: Grandpa Vincenzo Mandola, Uncle Charlie Corona, Uncle Frank Lamonte in the late 40's at Joe Mandola's farm in Tomball, Texas.

Tomato and Mozzarella Salad

Tomato and Mozzarella Salad

Insalata di Pomodori e Mozzarella

SERVES 6–8

6	cups cherry tomatoes, preferably orange, yellow and red, halved
1/2	cup extra-virgin olive oil
1/4	cup aged balsamic vinegar
1/2	pound (225 g) fresh mozzarella cheese, store-bought or homemade (see page 175), cut into pieces the same size as cherry tomatoes
	Kosher salt and freshly-ground black pepper
1/2	cup Basil Pesto (see page 174)
6	large basil leaves, for garnish
	Rustic Italian bread, sliced

TO PREPARE

1 In a large salad or mixing bowl, toss the cherry tomatoes with the olive oil and the balsamic vinegar.
2 Add the mozzarella and salt and pepper to taste, and toss. Marinate for two to three minutes.

To serve

Arrange the salad on a large serving platter or individual serving plates. Drizzle with the pesto and garnish with the basil leaves. Serve with bread.

Now this is a twist on the classic dish *Caprese*, which is probably the most famous dish, and certainly the most famous salad, from the isle of Capri. –Damian

There is no trick to our recipe. Just always use the best of everything you can find. –Johnny

It's a typical Italian dish—it all depends on the earth. –Damian

From left to right: Great-Grandma Bessie Palazzo, Aunt Bonnie Palazzo Zarzana, Great-Grandpa John C. Palazzo, Nita Palazzo Carrabba, Great-Great-Grandmother Nita Palazzo.

Escarole Salad
Insalata di Scarola

SERVES 4

VINAIGRETTE INGREDIENTS

1 clove garlic, peeled and minced
1/4 cup Champagne vinegar
2 teaspoons Dijon mustard
Kosher salt and freshly-ground black pepper
3/4 cup extra-virgin olive oil

SALAD INGREDIENTS

1 head escarole, torn into large pieces
1 small bunch arugula
1/2 cup shaved Parmesan cheese

We sure lived on my mother's wonderful escarole salads. –Damian

Escarole is a big time Mediterranean green. –Johnny

My mother didn't use champagne vinegar in her escarole salad, but we encourage you to go for it here. You'll be happy you did. –Damian

And the escarole is not only used in salads like this. It can also be sautéed or braised. –Johnny

If you want to add a little sweetness to the flavor, whisk in a couple teaspoons of honey to the vinaigrette, or you can toss thinly sliced Granny Smith apples and toasted pecans in with the salad. –Damian

TO PREPARE

1 In a mixing bowl, whisk together the garlic and vinegar and let sit for 30 minutes.
2 Add the Dijon mustard and salt and pepper to taste. Slowly whisk in the olive oil until fully incorporated.
3 Add the greens to the bowl and toss well with the vinaigrette to coat evenly.

To serve
Arrange the salad on individual serving plates or in a large salad bowl. Top with the shaved Parmesan cheese. Leftover vinaigrette can be stored for one week in the refrigerator.

Caesar Salad
Insalata Cesare

SERVES 2

CROUTON INGREDIENTS

1   cup cubed Italian or French bread, 3/4-inch (2 cm) cubes

2   tablespoons extra-virgin olive oil

1   medium garlic clove, peeled
     Kosher salt

1   tablespoon grated Parmigiano Reggiano cheese

SALAD INGREDIENTS

2   heads fresh romaine lettuce

1/3   cup extra-virgin olive oil
     Kosher salt

2   medium garlic cloves, peeled

5   anchovy filets, chopped fine

1   tablespoon small capers

1/4   teaspoon dry mustard

1   egg, separated
     Juice of 1/2 lemon

2   tablespoons red wine vinegar
     Dash of Worcestershire sauce
     Dash of Tabasco

3   tablespoons grated Parmigiano Reggiano cheese
     Fresh black pepper

Let's hear it for an Italian guy who made good—one Signore Cardini who invented this salad in, of all places, Tijuana, Mexico. –Johnny

At my old restaurant called Damian's, we made Caesar salads tableside, and we made a lot of them. Sometimes, I'd spend all night going from one table to another making Caesar salads. The place was backed up like planes at LaGuardia. –Damian

TO PREPARE THE CROUTONS

1   Crush the garlic clove with the flat side of a chef's knife. Place the garlic and 2 tablespoons of the olive oil in a small skillet and place skillet over a moderate heat.

2   When the garlic starts to turn brown discard and add the bread cubes to the skillet, cook and toss until the bread is golden and crispy. Drain on paper towels and while still hot season with salt and toss with a tablespoon of Parmigiano Reggiano cheese.

TO PREPARE THE SALAD

1   Remove outer leaves of romaine lettuce until you reach the heart. Use outer leaves for another salad. Wash the romaine hearts and dry well. Place the lettuce in a kitchen cloth and refrigerate to make sure it will be dry and cold when ready to toss.

2   In a large wooden bowl, sprinkle about a 1/2 teaspoon of salt, and add about 1 teaspoon of olive oil. With two forks, take the 2 garlic cloves, break in half and using one of the forks, rub the bowl with the cut side of one of the halves of the garlic, rubbing it through the olive oil and salt to "season"

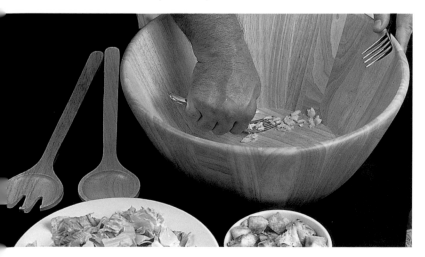

[Continued]

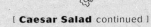

INSALATE E ZUPPE

the bowl. Then mash all of the garlic with the back of your forks until it is combined with the olive oil and salt to form a smooth paste.

3   Add the anchovies and capers and mash with your forks into the garlic mixture.

4   Add the dry mustard and the yolk from the egg with a little bit of the egg white into the bowl and mix well into the paste.

5   Now with a wooden spoon start adding the remaining olive oil into the bowl, a little at a time, stirring constantly in the same direction with the spoon until you have a nice creamy base.

6   Add the lemon juice, vinegar, Worcestershire, Tabasco and 1 tablespoon of Parmigiano Reggiano cheese. Mix well.

7   Tear lettuce into bite size pieces and toss with the dressing. Grind fresh black pepper over lettuce and toss again. Add croutons. Toss only a few times so croutons won't get soggy.

To serve

Serve on large chilled dinner plates. Sprinkle with the remaining Parmigiano Reggiano cheese before serving salad. Offer more freshly-ground black pepper. Salad should be eaten right away.

I think I am most proud of Damian for two things in his life. One was getting picked Altar Boy of the Year in eighth grade. The other was winning Best Caesar Salad in the Houston Caesar Salad Contest. –Johnny

Damian receiving the Altar Boy of the Year award.

Mamma's Mixed Tossed Salad
Mamma's Insalata Mista

SERVES 6–8

VINAIGRETTE INGREDIENTS

3 tablespoons red wine vinegar

Kosher salt and freshly-ground black pepper

A pinch of dried oregano

3/4 teaspoon chopped fresh basil

1/4 teaspoon finely-chopped garlic

1/2 cup + 1 tablespoon extra-virgin olive oil

SALAD INGREDIENTS

8 cups mixed lettuce greens, washed, dried and torn into bite-sized pieces

1 small cucumber, peeled and cut in half lengthwise, seeded, cut into 1/8-inch (3 mm) slices

1 celery heart, sliced 1/4-inch (6 mm) thick, with leaves

1 medium tomato, seeded and diced

1/2 small red onion, peeled and sliced

10 green Sicilian olives, pitted and sliced into julienne strips

10 Calamata olives, pitted and julienned

4 tablespoons grated Parmesan cheese, optional

TO PREPARE

1 In a mixing bowl, whisk together all the vinaigrette ingredients except the olive oil. Slowly whisk in the olive oil until fully incorporated.

2 Place all the salad ingredients except the Parmesan cheese in a salad bowl and toss well with enough vinaigrette to coat evenly.

To serve

Arrange the salad on individual serving plates and top each one with the grated Parmesan cheese, if desired. Leftover vinaigrette can be stored in the refrigerator for one week.

My mother always made great mixed salads. You just have to use your imagination to come up with great combinations of your own. We use our Italian creativity.

—Damian

The salads I remember were all really simple and they always tasted so good.

—Johnny

Johnny's Taco Salad
Insalata Mexicana

SERVES 4–6

TACO MEAT INGREDIENTS

2	tablespoons vegetable oil
2	medium white onions, peeled and finely chopped
4	cloves garlic, peeled and minced
2	pounds (900 g) ground beef chuck
2	teaspoons chile powder
1	teaspoon ground cumin
1	teaspoon dried oregano
1/2	teaspoon cayenne pepper
	Kosher salt and freshly-ground pepper

SALAD INGREDIENTS

	Vegetable or peanut oil for frying tortillas
6	8-inch (20 cm) flour tortillas or 4 store-bought flour tortilla bowls
1	head iceberg lettuce, shredded
1	large tomato, cored and diced
2	cups grated Monterey Jack cheese
1	cup sour cream
2	small to medium avocados, peeled, pitted and diced
	Corn chips (optional, as much or as little as you like)

TO PREPARE THE TACO MEAT

1 Heat the oil in a large skillet over medium heat. Add the onion and garlic, and sauté for two minutes, until translucent. Add the beef and stir to break it up. Cook for about 10 minutes or until browned.

2 Stir in the chile powder, cumin, oregano, cayenne powder, salt and pepper to taste and continue cooking for two more minutes. Remove from the heat and set aside.

My Aunt Bessie got this recipe out of the newspaper, and she made it a lot when we were little. She and my grandmother would put this dish together, and we kids couldn't get enough of it. –Johnny

I didn't eat taco salads growing up. But I sure ate tacos. And it's the same thing, pretty much. Either way you prefer to eat it; it's good. –Damian

For extra flavor and crunch, I like to add a few layers of crushed corn chips. –Johnny

TO PREPARE THE TORTILLA SHELL

1 Preheat the oil to 350° F (180° C) in a heavy 4-quart (3.75 l) Dutch oven. You will need at least five to six inches (13 to 15 cm) of oil.

2 Use a large ladle and push each tortilla down in the oil, holding it in place with the ladle. The sides will naturally turn upward to form a bowl as long as you keep the tortilla submerged in the center with the ladle. It will take about four minutes until they are lightly browned.

3 Cool the tortillas before making the salads. You can make these shells a day ahead of time if you wish. Cool them and store in an airtight container.

To serve

Place a tortilla shell on a plate. Layer first with 1/4 of the shredded lettuce, diced tomato and hot taco meat. Repeat two more times. Top with a little more lettuce, Monterey Jack cheese, a dollop of sour cream, diced avocado and diced tomato.

Roasted Radicchio Salad
Insalata di Radicchio Arrosto

SERVES 4

DRESSING INGREDIENTS
1/4   cup balsamic vinegar
1/2   cup extra-virgin olive oil
3   roasted garlic cloves (see page 180)
8   green olives, pitted and roughly chopped
      Kosher salt and freshly-ground black pepper

SALAD INGREDIENTS
4   radicchio heads, halved, keeping the cores intact
1/4   cup olive oil
3   tablespoons balsamic vinegar
      Kosher salt and freshly-ground black pepper
1   tablespoon chopped Italian parsley

TO PREPARE

1 Preheat the oven to 450° F (230° C).

2 Lay the radicchio on a large baking sheet and drizzle with the olive oil, balsamic vinegar, and salt and pepper to taste. Roast in the oven for six minutes, then flip and cook an additional three minutes.

3 In a mixing bowl, whisk together all dressing ingredients.

4 Remove the radicchio from the oven and transfer to a serving platter. Drizzle with the dressing while the radicchio is still hot.

To serve

Sprinkle with chopped Italian parsley and serve warm or at room temperature.

Treviso is a town outside of Venice that grows a kind of radicchio that is long instead of round. In the States radicchio has become known simply as *treviso*. —Damian

It tastes good cooked all kinds of ways, but especially roasted or grilled, it has a real smooth flavor. —Johnny

It's a wonderful side dish for a roast or maybe some kind of hearty stew. —Damian

35

Arugala Salad

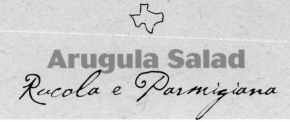

Arugula Salad
Rucola e Parmigiana

SERVES 4

VINAIGRETTE INGREDIENTS

2	tablespoons red wine vinegar
	Kosher salt and freshly-ground black pepper
	A pinch of dried oregano
1	teaspoon chopped fresh basil
1/2	teaspoon finely-chopped garlic
6	tablespoons extra-virgin olive oil

SALAD INGREDIENTS

2	bunches arugula leaves, washed and drained
4	radishes, washed, ends trimmed and sliced thin
1/2	cup shaved Parmesan cheese
1/4	cup toasted pinenuts (see page 180)

TO PREPARE

1 In a mixing bowl, whisk together all the vinaigrette ingredients except the olive oil. Slowly pour in the olive oil while whisking until it is fully incorporated.

2 Add the arugula and radishes to a salad bowl and toss well with enough vinaigrette to coat evenly.

To serve

Arrange the salad on individual serving plates and top each one with the shaved Parmesan cheese and pinenuts. Leftover vinaigrette can be stored for one week in the refrigerator.

Arugula, in the national renaissance of Italian cooking, has became one of our really great greens. –Damian

Damian once did a variation of this salad with goat cheese and hazelnuts. We took it off the menu 12 years ago and people still ask for it. –Johnny

Italian Coleslaw
Insalata di Cavolo

SERVES 4–6

VINAIGRETTE INGREDIENTS

3   roasted garlic cloves, mashed to a
     consistency of paste (see page 180)

$^1/_2$ lemon, juiced

$^1/_4$ cup red wine vinegar

$^1/_2$ teaspoon dried oregano

     Kosher salt and freshly-ground black pepper

$^1/_2$ cup extra-virgin olive oil

COLESLAW INGREDIENTS

$^1/_2$ large head green cabbage, cored and grated

$^1/_2$ large fennel bulb, grated

1   large carrot, julienned

$^1/_4$ cup Italian parsley, coarsely chopped

$^1/_2$ small red onion, julienned

TO PREPARE

1   In a mixing bowl, whisk together the mashed garlic, lemon juice, red wine vinegar, oregano, and salt and pepper to taste. Slowly whisk in the olive oil until fully incorporated.

2   Combine all the coleslaw ingredients in a large salad bowl and then pour over enough vinaigrette to coat evenly.

3   Refrigerate the salad for about an hour, tossing it a few times so the flavors will all come together. Serve well chilled

To serve
This salad goes great with fried chicken and mashed potatoes.

We ate coleslaw a lot growing up. –Johnny

Nowadays we call the dressing vinaigrette, but in those days we didn't call it anything. It was just what we had. –Damian

It kind of cleanses your palate. –Johnny

When my mother said, "Dress the salad," nobody at our house said, "Do you want Thousand Island or Ranch?" –Damian

Mamma's Pasta with Pea Soup
Mamma's Pasta con Piseddi

SERVES 6–8

1	large onion, peeled and chopped fine
4	tablespoons extra-virgin olive oil
4	cloves garlic, peeled and minced
1	10-ounce (300 g) can crushed tomatoes or 1 cup cherry tomatoes, quartered
1/2	cup chopped Italian parsley
1/2	tablespoon chopped fresh mint
2 1/2	cups store-bought or homemade Chicken Stock (see page 166)
1	10-ounce (300 g) package frozen peas, thawed or 10 ounces (300 g) fresh peas

	Kosher salt and freshly-ground black pepper
1	cup fusili pasta
	Extra-virgin olive oil for garnish
	Grated Pecorino Romano cheese, for garnish

TO PREPARE

1 In a soup pot, sauté the onion in the olive oil until soft. Add the garlic and cook for one minute. Add the tomatoes, parsley and mint and cook until the tomatoes thicken, about three to four minutes.

2 Add the chicken stock and peas, season lightly with salt and pepper, and simmer for about 30 minutes.

3 About 10 minutes before serving, bring a pot of water to a boil and season lightly with salt. Add the ditalini pasta, cook about halfway and then drain, reserving one to two cups of the pasta water.

4 To finish, add the drained pasta and enough of the reserved pasta water to the first pot to make a soupy consistency. Adjust the seasoning and bring back to a simmer. Continue at a simmer until the fusili is done.

To serve

Ladle the soup into individual bowls and garnish with a drizzle of the olive oil and grated Pecorino Romano cheese.

My mother came by the house yesterday with pasta and peas for my little son. He loved it. –Johnny

This is so simple, so satisfying. We usually had this pasta soup with peas on a Friday, when, like the rest of the Catholics in the U.S. we weren't eating meat. And with this soup we didn't miss the meat, either. –Damian

Minestrone Soup

Minestrone Soup
Minestrone

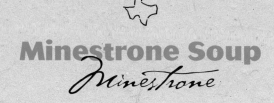

SERVES 6–8

2/3 cup dried cannellini beans, soaked overnight in water with a pinch of baking soda, drained and rinsed

8 cups water

1 bay leaf

5 cloves garlic, peeled

1 dried red chile

4 tablespoons olive oil

2 small onions peeled and diced

1 large leek, white and green parts sliced thinly

1 teaspoon dried oregano

2 celery ribs, diced

2 small carrots, diced

1 medium zucchini, diced

1 12-ounce (350 g) can whole tomatoes, chopped with juice

1 tablespoon tomato paste

1 Parmesan rind, about 6 x 2 inches (15 x 5 cm)

1 1/2 cups chopped kale or chard leaves

Kosher salt and freshly-ground black pepper

1/4 cup Basil Pesto, store-bought or homemade (see page 174), for garnish

Extra-virgin olive oil for garnish

Grated Parmesan, for garnish

TO PREPARE

1 Place the rinsed beans in a small pot with 5 cups of the water, bay leaf, 1 clove of the garlic and the red chile. Bring to a boil then turn the heat down and cook with the lid slightly ajar. When the beans are just tender, take off the heat and set aside, leaving them in their own liquid. Remove and discard chile.

2 Meanwhile, heat the olive oil in a Dutch oven set on medium-high heat. Add the onions and leek and cook about four minutes. Add the dried oregano, minced garlic, celery and carrots, and cook another two minutes. Then add the zucchini and cook an additional three minutes.

3 Add the tomatoes and the tomato paste and cook five minutes. Reduce the heat to low, add the beans and their liquid, 3 more cups of water and the Parmesan rind and cook for one hour.

4 To finish, add the kale, cook on medium-high heat for approximately five minutes, or until kale is tender. Add salt and pepper to taste.

To serve

Remove bay leaf and Parmesan rind from soup. Ladle the soup into bowls and garnish with the pesto, a drizzle of olive oil and the grated cheese.

Monday night was soup night in our family—maybe the same way Monday is red beans and rice night in New Orleans. You know, something simple in one pot after cooking a big Sunday dinner. –Johnny

My mother also made Minestrone with soup bones or beef shanks. My brother-in-law, Rocco, would take that beef right out of the minestrone. Rocco would eat the soup, sure. But then he'd douse the meat with Worcestershire and eat it with crackers. Nothing wrong with Rocco's taste! –Damian

There's no beef in this recipe, but for another layer of flavor you can sauté a 1/4 cup of diced pancetta and add it before the onions. –Johnny

You can also substitute 3 cups chicken stock instead of the remaining 3 cups of water. –Damian

Mamma's Bean Soup with Pasta
Mamma's Pasta e Fagioli

SERVES 4

2   cups dried white kidney beans, soaked overnight in water with a pinch of baking soda, drained and rinsed

2   tablespoons olive oil

3   ounces (90 g) pancetta, diced

1/2 large red onion, peeled and chopped

2   stalks celery, diced

2   teaspoons finely-chopped fresh rosemary

1   teaspoon dried oregano

4   cloves garlic, peeled and minced

1   bay leaf

2   cups store-bought or homemade Chicken Stock (see page 166)

6   ounces (175 g) crushed tomatoes

   Kosher salt and freshly-ground black pepper

2   cups broken buccatini pasta

2   cups pasta cooking water, reserved for beans

   Extra-virgin olive oil for garnish

   Grated Parmesan cheese, for garnish

TO PREPARE

1 In a 3-quart (2.75 l) stock pot, heat the olive oil over medium heat. Add the diced pancetta and sauté until crisp. Remove the pancetta, leaving the oil in the pot, and drain the pancetta on a paper towel.

2 Add the red onion to the same stockpot and sauté on medium for three minutes. Add the celery and cook for two more minutes. Add the rosemary, oregano, garlic and bay leaf and cook for another five minutes.

3 Add the chicken stock, tomatoes, pancetta and the rinsed beans. Bring to a boil, then lower the heat. Season with salt and pepper and simmer until beans are tender, two to three hours, partially covered.

4 When the beans are tender, adjust seasoning. Boil the pasta to al dente in lightly-salted water. Drain and reserve 2 cups of the water.

5 To finish, add the cooked pasta and enough reserved pasta water to the soup to make "soupy".

To serve

Ladle the soup into individual bowls and garnish with the extra-virgin olive oil and grated Parmesan cheese.

Every Italian worth his salt has to make a *pasta e fagioli*. There are as many recipes for this in Italy and among Italian-Americans as there are spaghetti sauces. –Damian

I remember the first trip I took to Tuscany. That was the first time I got on a real *pasta e fagioli* kick. It was just so simple and so good. –Johnny

Potato and Onion Soup
Zuppa di Patate e Cipolle

SERVES 6

3   tablespoons butter

3   tablespoons extra-virgin olive oil

1 1/2 pounds (750 g) yellow onions, peeled and very thinly sliced

     Kosher salt and freshly-grated black pepper

3 1/2 cups store-bought or homemade Beef Stock (see page 166)

2   pounds (900 g) boiling potatoes, peeled and diced into 1/4-inch (6 mm) cubes

3   tablespoons freshly-grated Parmesan cheese

TO PREPARE

1 In a large skillet, melt the butter and oil over medium heat. Cook the onion with salt to taste until it softens and turns light brown. Remove from the heat and set aside.

2 In a 2-quart (2 l) pot, bring 3 cups of the beef stock to a boil on medium-high heat. Add the diced potatoes and boil until soft. Turn the heat down to low and add the wilted onions, simmering for 10 minutes. Season with salt and pepper.

3 If necessary, thin the soup with the remaining 1/2 cup of stock.

To serve

Ladle the soup into individual serving bowls. Pass the grated fresh Parmesan cheese around for people to sprinkle on top to their liking.

I love all onion soups, and this is one of the best of the bunch. It's delicious. It's hearty. And you can mix in all kinds of different onions and leeks, letting the potatoes bring a certain creaminess to the bowl. –Damian

Boy, that's good! –Johnny

43

Lee Ditta (right) with customer (left)

Side Dishes
Verdura e Pane

Our families made a lot of their best side dishes from vegetables that grew fresh in the rich soil and humid air of the Texas Gulf Coast. Beyond starting with something good, the only real trick is not to screw it up. Don't over-cook it, unless you have some super old-fashioned recipe in mind. And please don't cover it up with too many sauces or spices.

Traditional Sicilian recipes show a good deal of respect for quality ingredients—probably the doff of a peasant's cap to a thing he doesn't enjoy often enough. Some of the spirit of those early recipes comes through, we think, in these great side dish recipes—and in the photos on these pages.

One photo shows Lee Ditta, who sold produce and is one of our Sicilian cousins that lived right around the block from our family in the east end. This is back in the days when he carted his vegetables and fruits around on a horse-drawn carriage. He came right to your house in those days, sold you what you needed, and moved on. After some years, Mr. Ditta worked his way up to a truck. In the other photo, you see Johnny's great-grandmother Josephine Boss Carrabba, along with her sisters. It's a great picture for our side dish chapter, since these good ladies farmed in the Brazos River bottom. Farming was always real good there!

"The Boss Sisters":
Lena DeLuke, Rosie Rizzo,
Great Grandma Josie Carrabba
and Angelina Mauro

Stuffed Rolled Eggplant
Involtini di Melanzane

VERDURA E PANE

3 medium eggplants
Kosher salt
Vegetable oil for frying
4 ounces (115 g) Fontina cheese, shredded
4 ounces (115 g) Pecorino Romano cheese, grated
2 cups whole milk ricotta cheese

2 cups cherry tomatoes, washed and cut in half lengthwise
1 tablespoon peeled and minced garlic
3 tablespoons coarsely-chopped Italian parsley
2 tablespoons extra-virgin olive oil
1 tablespoon balsamic vinegar
Kosher salt and freshly-ground black pepper

TO PREPARE

1 Slice the eggplants lengthwise about ¹/₂-inch (1.5 cm) thick. Salt the slices on both sides and place in a colander with a weighted plate on top and with a pan underneath to catch draining juices. Let them sweat for 20 minutes then pat dry.

2 In a large sauté pan, pour in about two inches (5 cm) of vegetable oil and preheat on medium high until it is almost smoking.

3 Fry the eggplant slices in a single layer without crowding—one or two at a time, depending on the size of the pan. Fry them quickly, about one to two minutes until lightly browned, and drain on fresh paper towels to absorb the excess oil. Let the eggplant cool. Pour in more oil for frying if necessary for the remainder.

4 Mix together in a bowl the Fontina, Pecorino Romano and ricotta cheese. Season to taste with salt and pepper. Set aside.

5 Preheat the oven to 375° F (190° C).

6 Place about 1 rounded tablespoon of the cheese mixture at the fattest end of the eggplant and roll up to form a small bundle. Place the rolls in a 9 x 13-inch (23 x 33 cm) casserole dish, being careful not to overlap them.

7 Toss together in a mixing bowl the tomatoes, garlic, parsley, olive oil, balsamic vinegar and salt and pepper to taste. Then distribute the topping evenly over the eggplant rolls.

8 Bake for 20 minutes, or until the cheese is melted and oozing out of the sides.

To serve

Remove the eggplant from the oven and serve hot or at room temperature, family-style.

My aunt Margarite Mandola Lampasas is a great lady and her rolled eggplant is the best. –Damian

There are all sorts of things you can stuff eggplant with. When the family got together, just about everybody brought some kind of stuffed and rolled eggplant. –Johnny

Eggplant Stuffed with Garlic and Pecorino in Tomato Sauce

Melanzane Ripieno con Aglio e Pecorino in Sugo

SERVES 6–8

TOMATO SAUCE INGREDIENTS

3/4	cup olive oil
1	large onion, peeled and minced
1/4	cup peeled and finely-chopped garlic cloves
4	tablespoons tomato paste
3	28-ounce (790 g) cans whole tomatoes, chopped
1	cup fresh basil leaves, torn into small pieces
	Kosher salt and freshly-ground black pepper

EGGPLANT INGREDIENTS

6	Japanese eggplant or small baby eggplant
1/2	cup peeled and thinly-sliced garlic cloves
1/2	cup Pecorino Romano pieces, cut into 1/2- to 3/4-inch (1.5–2 cm) pieces, about the same size as the garlic clove slices
1 1/2	cups vegetable oil
1	tablespoon chopped parsley
	Cooked pasta (optional)

TO PREPARE THE TOMATO SAUCE

1 Heat the olive oil in a large saucepan on medium heat. Add the onion and cook for two minutes. Add the chopped garlic and cook for another four to five minutes until onions are soft. Add the tomato paste and cook for two minutes until thick and slightly darkened.

2 Add the tomatoes and cook another 20 minutes, stirring frequently. Stir in the basil and salt and pepper to taste. Turn the heat down to low and simmer for about three minutes.

TO PREPARE THE EGGPLANT AND FINISH THE DISH

1 Make slits in each eggplant with a small knife going all the way around. Stuff slices of garlic and Pecorino Romano cheese in each slit.

2 Heat the vegetable oil in a cast iron skillet on high heat. Brown the whole eggplants on all sides, about 10 to 15 minutes. Transfer to a paper towel and drain.

3 Place the drained, fried eggplants in the pan with the Tomato Sauce. Cook on medium-low heat until soft and tender, about 10 to 15 minutes. Add a little water if needed so sauce doesn't get too thick.

To serve

Transfer the eggplant to a platter and garnish with chopped parsley. Serve eggplant as a side dish or with your favorite pasta.

Sicilians cook eggplant thousands of ways. This is one way my Grandma Testa fixed it. –Damian

Yeah, I love this dish with some rigatoni. –Johnny

You can use this tomato sauce here or drop the fried eggplant in Mamma's Sunday Sugo (see page 120). –Damian

Stewed Peppers
Peperonata

SERVES 4–6

3 tablespoons extra-virgin olive oil
1/2 large red onion, peeled and sliced thin
1 red bell pepper, julienned 1/2-inch wide
1 yellow bell pepper, julienned 1/2-inch wide
1 green bell pepper, julienned 1/2-inch wide
2 cloves garlic, peeled and crushed (but left whole)
3 tablespoons Mamma's Pomodoro "Tomato Sauce" (see page 173)
   Kosher salt and freshly-ground black pepper
10 fresh basil leaves, julienned, for garnish

TO PREPARE

1 In a large sauté pan, heat the olive oil on medium-high heat until it sizzles, about two minutes. Add the onions and cook until they start to caramelize slightly, about four to five minutes.

2 Turn the heat down to low and add the peppers and crushed garlic cloves. Continue to cook for a few minutes until peppers soften.

3 Add the tomato sauce and salt and pepper to taste, and cook 15 minutes with the pan covered. Remove the lid and cook another 20 minutes until peppers are soft and caramelized.

To serve

Sprinkle on the fresh basil before serving. This is also great in a sandwich made with Mamma's Bread (see page 170).

When I think of this dish, I think about my dad's Italian sausage. Sausage and peppers sure do go hand in hand. –Johnny

You can do all kinds of things with this. You can bake it with potatoes, toss it with pasta or serve it as part of an antipasto.
–Damian

And don't forget that famous Roman dish, *Pollo ai Peperoni*, chicken with peppers. This can be the base for that. –Johnny

Stuffed Artichokes
Carciofi Ripieni

SERVES 4

4	whole artichokes, cleaned and trimmed
1	tablespoon kosher salt
1	teaspoon freshly-ground black pepper
$1/2$	cup extra-virgin olive oil
2	cups Mamma's Breadcrumbs (see page 171)

SIDE DISHES

TO PREPARE

1 First, cut $3/4$ inch (2 cm) off the top of the artichoke. Then cut most of the stem off, leaving $1/4$-inch (6 mm) stem (make sure to cut the stem flat and level so the artichoke will be able to stand on its own in the baking pan).

2 Trim remaining leaf tips with scissors so each leaf tip is perfectly horizontal.

3 Soak artichokes in lemon and water, with artichokes totally submerged until ready to stuff. This will keep the artichokes from turning brown.

4 Add enough olive oil to breadcrumbs to moisten. Remove an artichoke from the water and drain water by turning upside-down. Pry open leaves and fill between each leaf with about 1 teaspoon of stuffing mixture. Do not overstuff.

5 Place stuffed artichokes in a pot just large enough so they fit snugly and fill with about one inch (2.5 cm) of water or just to the bottom of the artichoke. Season water with salt and black pepper. Drizzle 1 tablespoon of olive oil over each of the stuffed artichokes.

6 Place pot on top of stove and bring to a boil. Reduce to a simmer and cover pot. Baste artichokes lightly after $1/2$ hour of cooking with liquid in the pot. Continue cooking until leaves pull easily from stem, about another 30 to 45 minutes. (Do not boil the artichokes, steam gently or you will boil all the stuffing out of them.)

To serve

These are best served warm but are also good after they have cooled.

Here's a dish every Sicilian knows and loves. Stuffed Artichokes are special to our hearts. –Damian

And they're fun to eat, you know. I like nibbling the stuffing right off the leaves. –Johnny

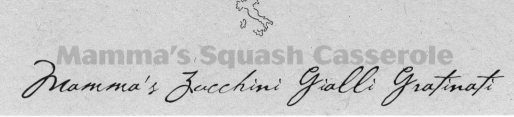
SERVES 4–6

- ¼ cup extra-virgin olive oil
- 1 medium onion, peeled and chopped
- 1 large celery rib, thinly sliced
- 4 cloves garlic, peeled and chopped fine
- 2 pounds (900 g) yellow squash, ends trimmed, sliced ¼-inch (6 mm) thick
- 1 cup store-bought seasoned breadcrumbs or Mamma's Breadcrumbs (see page 171)
- 2 tablespoons chopped fresh parsley
- 2 green onions, sliced into small rings
- Kosher salt and freshly-ground black pepper
- ¼ cup finely-grated Pecorino Romano cheese
- 2 eggs
- ½ cup unseasoned breadcrumbs
- ¼ stick butter for dotting

This is a great summer dish when squash is at its peak. –Damian

You know, you see this dish all over the southern United States, but Grandma put her Sicilian twist on it. –Johnny

I love this with roasted chicken or pork.

–Damian

TO PREPARE

1 Preheat the oven to 400° (200° C).

2 Lightly butter an 8-inch (20 cm) glass pie pan or gratin pan.

3 Heat olive oil in a 12-inch (30 cm) skillet, add onion and cook until it starts to turn golden brown. Add celery, garlic and sliced squash. Cook until squash is very soft and pan juices are almost dry. Transfer mixture to a bowl and let cool.

4 To the bowl of cooled squash, add Mamma's Breadcrumbs, parsley, green onions, salt, pepper, cheese and eggs. Mix well.

5 Spread the squash mixture evenly in the prepared pie pan or gratin pan. Sprinkle with unseasoned breadcrumbs. Dot with butter. Bake 20 minutes or until lightly browned.

To serve
Serve family-style with any meat, poultry or seafood entrée.

Mandola Baked Beans
Fagioli Mandola

SERVES 4–6

6   ounces (175 g) salt pork, cut into 1¹/₂ x ³/₄-inch (4 x 2 cm) pieces
1   pound (450 g) navy beans, soaked overnight and drained
1   small yellow onion, peeled and finely diced
¹/₂ cup ketchup
¹/₄ cup packed dark brown sugar
3   teaspoons Dijon mustard
¹/₄ teaspoon cayenne pepper
2   whole cloves
1   cup boiling water
2   tablespoons butter
1   small yellow, onion, peeled and sliced
1   small red bell pepper, cut into medium julienne
1   small green bell pepper, cut into medium julienne
    Kosher salt and freshly-ground black pepper
1   pound (450 g) medium-sharp cheddar cheese, shredded

TO PREPARE

1 Preheat the oven to 300° F (150° C).

2 Blanch the pieces of salt pork in boiling water for five minutes to remove some of the saltiness. Drain and rinse well under cold running water.

3 Place the beans in a large pot or flameproof casserole. Add the blanched salt pork, diced onion, ketchup, brown sugar, mustard, cayenne pepper, cloves and boiling water.

4 Cover tightly and bake three to five hours, or until the beans are tender and the liquid has been reduced to a thick sauce. Check occasionally during the last couple of hours of baking and add additional boiling water, if beans become dry. When cooked, let the beans cool completely. Remove the cloves.

5 While the beans are cooking, prepare the finishing ingredients: heat the butter in a large sauté pan over medium heat to cook the sliced onion and both peppers. Season with salt and pepper to taste. Cook for about 15 minutes until quite soft.

6 To finish the beans, ladle ¹/₃ of the beans into the bottom of a casserole dish, top with half of the onion–pepper mixture and then half of the cheese. Season with salt and pepper. Repeat this layer again and top with the last third of the beans.

7 Turn the heat up to 350° F (180° C). Cover the casserole and bake for 30 minutes, or until the beans are bubbling hot.

To serve

Remove the lid, stir and serve piping hot!

We called these Mandola Beans because it was my mother's baked bean recipe. –Damian

People love these beans! –Johnny

SIDE DISHES

Nonna Testa's Green Beans

Nonna Testa's Green Beans
Fagiolini della Nonna Testa

SERVES 4–6

1   pound (450 g) green beans, trimmed, cut in 2-inch (5 cm) lengths
1/4 cup extra-virgin olive oil
1/2 cup Mamma's Breadcrumbs (see page 171)
1/4 cup Pecorino Romano cheese
     Kosher salt and freshly-ground black pepper

TO PREPARE

1 Preheat the oven to 400° F (200° C).

2 Prepare an ice water bath in a large bowl.

3 Fill an 8-quart (7.5 l) pot with 6 quarts (5.5 l) of water. Bring the water to a boil and add 2 tablespoons salt. Add the beans and cook for approximately three minutes or until beans are tender. Drain the beans and place in the ice water bath until cool.

4 Drain the cooled beans and place in a mixing bowl. Add the olive oil and toss the beans to coat. Add the breadcrumbs, Pecorino Romano cheese and salt and pepper to taste. Toss thoroughly to coat the beans.

5 Spread beans out in a 1¹/₂- to 2-quart (1.5 to 2 l) shallow baking dish, trying to arrange the beans facing the same direction as much as possible.

6 Bake in the oven for 20 minutes, or until the breadcrumbs are golden brown.

To serve

Remove the beans from the oven, drizzle with a little extra-virgin olive oil if you wish and serve hot in the same baking dish, family-style.

This was a Sunday-type dish at our house. We never had this during the week. It was served after the pasta with the roast.
–Johnny

I wasn't a big vegetable eater. But let me tell you, this is a great way to get your kids to eat their vegetables. –Damian

Damian's brother-in-law, Johnny's uncle and godfather, Rocco Vallone, an early 40's cowboy.

53

SERVES 6

¹/₂ pound (225 g) dried cannellini beans, soaked overnight in water with a pinch of baking soda, drained and rinsed

4 tablespoons extra-virgin olive oil

2 ounces (60 g) pancetta or bacon, diced ¹/₄-inch thick

¹/₂ yellow onion, peeled and chopped fine

¹/₂ medium carrot, peeled and diced fine

1 large clove garlic, peeled and minced

1 teaspoon dried oregano

1 bay leaf

1 teaspoon kosher salt

¹/₄ teaspoon freshly-ground black pepper

3¹/₂ cups water

¹/₃ cup chopped fresh Italian parsley

Well, if it works for frijoles, it works for Italy's most famous beans. –Damian

And it's so easy, it's one of those recipes even the beginner can do. –Johnny

TO PREPARE

1 Heat 1 tablespoon of the olive oil in a large sauté pan on medium-high until it sizzles, about two minutes. Cook the pancetta until crisp, remove it with a slotted spoon and drain on paper towels.

2 In the same sauté pan, add the onion and carrot and cook for three minutes. Add the garlic, oregano, bay leaf and salt and pepper, stirring often so the garlic doesn't brown, cook another two minutes. Add the beans, water, parsley and the cooked pancetta.

3 Bring to a boil for five minutes, then turn down to low. Cook covered for 30 minutes. Remove the lid and cook another 1 to 1¹/₂ hours until the beans are tender. Smash the beans up with a wooden spoon until they have a somewhat pasty consistency.

4 In a sauté pan or iron skillet set over medium-high heat, heat the remaining olive oil until it sizzles. Add the smashed beans and cook until the oil is absorbed, continually stirring the beans. Add a little water if it gets too dry.

To serve

Best good and hot. Serve family-style.

Stewed Green Beans and New Potatoes
Fagiolini con Patatine in Umido

SERVES 8

2	tablespoons extra-virgin olive oil
2	slices pancetta or bacon, cut into medium slices
1/4	cup peeled and finely-chopped yellow onion
1	clove garlic, peeled and chopped fine
1	cup crushed canned tomatoes with juice
	Kosher salt and freshly-ground black pepper
1	pound (450 g) green beans, ends trimmed
16	very small new potatoes

TO PREPARE

1 Heat the oil and pancetta in a small pot over medium heat until the pancetta starts to render its fat.

2 Add the onion and cook until soft and starting to caramelize. Add the garlic and cook one minute more.

3 Add the tomatoes and bring to a boil. Season with salt and pepper to taste. Add the beans and potatoes and stir to coat.

4 Reduce the heat, cover and cook until beans and potatoes are tender about 20 minutes. Adjust the seasoning to taste.

To serve

This side dish is excellent with most meat, seafood and poultry entrees.

I'll speak for Johnny on this one. He loves this dish. It's so delicious! We used to have it with plain meat, like roast beef or a pork roast. –Damian

Just about anything tastes better when you cook it with pancetta and tomatoes.

–Johnny

Rosemary Roasted Potatoes

Rosemary Roasted Potatoes
Patate Arroste con Rosmarino

SERVES 6–8

3	pounds (1.4 kg) Yellow Finn or Yukon Gold potatoes, cut into six wedges each
2	tablespoons olive oil
	Kosher salt and freshly-ground black pepper
1	large yellow onion, peeled and julienned
2	tablespoons coarsely-chopped fresh rosemary

TO PREPARE

1 Preheat the oven to 450° F (230° C) and place an ovenproof shallow pan or cookie sheet with sides in the oven for 10 minutes.

2 Toss all of the ingredients together in a large bowl and set aside.

3 Once the pan or cookie sheet is hot, pull it out of the oven and spread the potatoes and onions evenly on the pan. Return to the oven and cook for 20 minutes.

4 Carefully turn the potatoes with a metal spatula, and cook another 20 to 30 minutes until potatoes are cooked through and golden brown.

To serve

Place in bowl and serve hot, family-style. A perfect side dish with any of the meat, poultry or seafood recipes in this book.

We've had a dish similar to these potatoes at Carrabba's since day one. They're real crunchy on the outside and fluffy on the inside. –Johnny

Everybody has always loved them! –Damian

57

Potato Celeriac Gratin
Gratinata di Patate e Sedano Rapa

SERVES 8

2   pounds (900 g) Yellow Finn or Yukon Gold potatoes, sliced 1/8-inch (3 mm) thick
2   small celeriac (celery root), peeled and sliced 1/8-inch (3 mm) thick
     Kosher salt and freshly-ground black pepper
2   cups caramelized onions or shallots (see page 182)
1   cup heavy cream
1   cup store-bought or homemade Chicken Stock (see page 166)
1 1/2 cups grated Parmigiano Reggiano cheese
4   tablespoons butter, cut into small cubes

TO PREPARE

1 Preheat the oven to 350° F (180° C).

2 Butter a 9 x 13-inch (23 x 33 cm) baking pan.

3 Layer the ingredients in this order, making a total of four layers: 1/2 of the potatoes, salt and pepper to taste, 1/4 of the caramelized onions, 1/4 of the cream, 1/4 of the stock, 1/4 of the Parmigiano Reggiano cheese and 1/4 of the butter dotted on top.

4 Do three more layers, alternating with the celeriac and potato slices.

5 Cover with foil and bake in the oven for 40 to 50 minutes.

6 Remove the foil and brown the top for an additional 15 to 20 minutes.

To serve
Remove the gratin from the oven and serve hot in the same dish, family-style.

Here's an Italian version of one of those delicious baked potato and cheese deals, kind of like au gratin and Lyonnaise. –Damian

Except better. The celery root adds a nice crunch, while the caramelized onions make it taste real sweet underneath the Parmigiano cheese. –Johnny

Mashed Potatoes with Mascarpone
Purea di Patate con Mascarpone

SERVES 4–6

2	pounds (900 g) russet potatoes, peeled and cut into quarters
7	tablespoons unsalted butter, softened
2 1/2	tablespoons mascarpone cheese
1	tablespoon kosher salt
1	teaspoon freshly-ground black pepper

TO PREPARE

1 Place the potatoes in a stockpot with enough cool water to cover them by two inches (5 cm).

2 Bring to a boil over a high heat and cook the potatoes until tender. This should take about 30 minutes after the water comes to a boil. Test the doneness by inserting a fork into the center of one of the potato pieces.

3 When the potatoes are done, drain and, working quickly, place the potatoes in the bowl of a mixer fitted with a wire whip. Add the softened butter and turn the mixer on low speed. Mix potatoes for 10 seconds and then add the mascarpone cheese.

4 Stop the machine and, with a spatula, scrape down the sides of the bowl. Add the salt and pepper to taste.

5 Turn the machine back on to medium speed and whip the potatoes well. If the potatoes are a little dry, add a little more mascarpone cheese. The potatoes should be creamy and fluffy—not too dry and not too runny.

To serve

Transfer the potatoes into a warm serving dish.

You know how things are nowadays—people are putting all sorts of weird things in mashed potatoes. But we loved mashed potatoes growing up, and we like, the simple old-fashioned potatoes. –Johnny

The mascarpone was all my idea. –Damian

That's okay, Damian. This is a really good twist on mashed potatoes. –Johnny

Pesto Potatoes

Pesto Potatoes
Patate con Pesto

SERVES 6

1	recipe Basil Pesto (see page 174)
2	pounds (900 g) Yellow Finn or Yukon Gold potatoes
	Kosher salt and freshly-ground black pepper

TO PREPARE

1 Prepare the pesto.

2 Boil the potatoes in salted water for approximately 35 minutes or until tender when pierced with a fork. Drain and peel them. Cut each of the potatoes into eight pieces.

3 Toss the potatoes with enough pesto to coat. Add salt and pepper to taste.

To serve

Great served with your favorite meat, poultry or seafood dish.

Pesto, with plenty of fresh basil, is good with any starch, not just with pasta. –Johnny

Yeah! And instead of traditional pine nuts you can use walnuts or a combination of both. –Damian

Or good old Texas pecans. –Johnny

When the pesto hits the hot potatoes, it releases the garlic and basil and all the other aromas. –Damian

You'll love it! –Johnny

French Fries
Patate Fritti

SERVES 4

1 1/2 pounds (24 ounces) Russet potatoes, peeled and cut into 1/2-inch (1.5 cm) square slices

Vegetable oil for frying

Fine sea salt to taste

TO PREPARE

1 Soak the potatoes in cold water for one hour to remove some starch.

2 Preheat vegetable oil to 330° F (175° C) in a large saucepan, about four to five inches (10–13 cm) deep.

3 Remove the potatoes from the water, dry off completely and fry in the oil, being careful not to splatter. Fry the potatoes for about four minutes until they are limp and about halfway cooked.

4 Remove from the oil and drain on paper towels. You may need to do this in two batches. Set the cooking oil aside, covered for future use.

5 Lay the potatoes out on a sheet pan and refrigerate for two hours or overnight, until completely chilled. At this point you may also freeze them if you wish and cook later.

6 Just before serving, reheat the oil to 365° F (185° C) and fry the chilled potatoes for two to three minutes or until golden brown and crisp. Drain on a paper-towel-lined sheet pan and, season with salt while still hot.

To serve

Serve immediately. Excellent with a nice salad and our Barbecue Beef Brisket or Grilled T-Bone (see page 90 and 93).

What's not to like about French Fries?
–Johnny

And there's even less not to like about these. Choosing older potatoes and soaking them in cold water gets rid of some of the starch. It's some chemistry thing. It gives you a lighter, fluffier potato. –Damian

Left to right: Uncle Frank Mandola, Uncle Sam Mandola, Papa Tony Mandola (Damian's father), Aunt Margaret Mandola, Uncle Joe Mandola, 1910.

Southern Baked Yams

SERVES 6

4	pounds (1.8 kg) yams or sweet potatoes, peeled and cut into wedges
	Kosher salt and freshly-ground black pepper
1/4	cup bourbon
1	cup orange juice
1/2	cup brown sugar
1/3	cup flour
3/4	cup chopped pecans
4	tablespoons butter, cut into cubes

TO PREPARE

1 Preheat the oven to 400° F (200° C).

2 Place the yams or sweet potatoes into a buttered 9 x 9-inch (23 x 23 cm) casserole dish and season with salt and pepper to taste. Drizzle with the bourbon and orange juice. Cover with foil and bake in the oven for 35 to 45 minutes until tender.

3 Remove from the oven and take off the foil. In a medium-sized bowl, mix together the brown sugar, flour and pecans.

4 Sprinkle the mixture evenly over the top of the cooked yams, dot with butter and return to the oven for 10 to 15 minutes until it's brown and bubbly.

To serve

While good and hot, serve family-style from the same casserole dish.

My mother always baked yams. She'd split them open and fill them with butter. –Damian

My grandmother was raised in Louisiana—and a lot of folks call these Louisiana yams. –Johnny

That's because they're actually sweet potatoes, not yams at all. –Damian

I don't care what they are, as long as I can have seconds at Thanksgiving. –Johnny

Fried Cardoons
Cardooni Fritti

SERVES 4–6

BATTER INGREDIENTS	
2	cups all-purpose flour
1	teaspoon baking powder
1	teaspoon kosher salt
1	teaspoon granulated garlic
1	egg, beaten
1	tablespoon extra-virgin olive oil
2¹/₂ cups milk	

CARDOON INGREDIENTS	
2	bunches cardoons (in season during the fall or may be available at farmers' markets)
1	lemon, halved, for cardoon water
	Vegetable or peanut oil for frying
	Kosher salt
	Lemon wedges for serving

TO PREPARE THE BATTER

1 Mix all the dry ingredients together in a mixing bowl.

2 Add the eggs and oil. With a wire whisk, gradually beat in the milk until you have the consistency of a medium-thick pancake batter. If the batter is too thick, add a little more milk. Set aside.

TO PREPARE THE CARDOONS

1 With a sharp knife, trim 1¹/₂ inches (4 cm) off the top and two inches (5 cm) from the bottom. Trim the strings off the ribs of the cardoons just as if you were trimming celery stalks and cut the cardoons into two-inch (5 cm) sticks. Place in a bowl of cold water with the lemon halves to keep them from turning brown.

2 Bring a large pot of salted water to a boil. Cook the cardoon sticks in the boiling water until they are tender and a knife inserts into them easily, about 10 to 15 minutes. Drain them and dry off any excess water. Let cool.

3 In a large pan, heat three to four inches (8–10 cm) of vegetable or peanut oil to 350° F (180° C).

4 Dip the cooked cardoons in the batter, shaking off any excess, and place about four at a time in the hot oil. Cook until golden brown, turning once, about two to three minutes. Place on a paper-towel-lined plate to drain.

To serve

Sprinkle with salt to taste while they are still hot. Serve with lemon wedges.

Cardoons are very popular in Italy and southern France. They look like a dull, green celery—but when you eat them, they taste almost like artichoke hearts, so of course Sicilians love them. –Damian

I remember at Thanksgiving and Christmas my grandmother used to fry them and fry them, and all the time she's frying, we're eating them right there in the kitchen. They hardly ever made it to the table! –Johnny

It was great stand-up food. You didn't feel right sitting down to eat cardooni. –Damian

⚐

Braised Fennel
Finocchio al Forno

SERVES 6

4	heads fennel, stalks removed and quartered
1/2	cup extra-virgin olive oil
	Kosher salt and freshly-ground black pepper
1/2	cup store-bought or homemade Chicken Stock (see page 166)
	Juice from 1/2 lemon
1/3	cup grated Parmigiano Reggiano cheese
2	tablespoons chopped fresh Italian parsley
4	tablespoons butter, cut into cubes

TO PREPARE

1 Preheat the oven to 400° F (200° C).

2 In a large bowl, toss the fennel quarters with the olive oil, salt and pepper to taste.

3 Place in a 9 x 13-inch (23 x 33 cm) casserole pan, cut-side-down. Pour in the chicken stock, cover with foil and bake in the oven for 35 to 45 minutes until tender.

4 Remove from the oven and take off the foil. Sprinkle on the lemon juice, cheese and parsley. Dot with the butter evenly on top and place back in the oven for 10 to 15 minutes until brown and bubbly.

To serve

Serve right from the casserole, good and hot.

Grandpa Mandola always had fennel at his table, and he always ate it raw. He said it was a good digestive. –Damian

And don't ever forget how good the seeds are in Italian sausage—right along with this braised version, drizzled with a little olive oil and lemon juice. –Johnny

Corn on the Cob with Sun-Dried Tomato Butter

Corn on the Cob with Sun-Dried Tomato Butter

Granoturco con Burro al Pomodori Secchi

SERVES 6

SEASONED BUTTER INGREDIENTS

1	4-ounce (113 g) stick butter, softened
1/3	cup oil-packed, sun-dried tomatoes, finely chopped
1	teaspoon tomato paste
1	teaspoon coarsely-chopped fresh oregano
1	tablespoon coarsely-chopped fresh basil
2	cloves garlic, peeled and minced
1	tablespoon kosher salt
1	tablespoon freshly-ground black pepper

CORN INGREDIENTS

6	ears of sweet corn
	Water for soaking

This is a Southern thing and a Texas thing, with kind of an Italian twist. –Damian

Once you spread sun-dried tomato butter on an ear of sweet corn, you'll want it this way every time. –Johnny

The sun-dried tomato butter is great on other foods as well, like vegetables, grilled or baked fish, or meats. –Damian

If you have any leftover butter just place it on a sheet of plastic wrap, roll it up, and refrigerate it until you're ready to use it again. –Johnny

TO PREPARE THE SEASONED BUTTER

Place the butter in a food processor or mixer and pulse a few times to soften. Add the remaining ingredients and mix until smooth and combined. Set aside.

TO PREPARE THE CORN ON THE COB

1 Pull back the husks on the corn and remove all the silk from each cob, but don't remove the husks. With the husks hanging from one end, place the cobs in a deep bowl filled with water and soak for a half hour.

2 Remove the cobs from the water, blot them with a paper towel and rub the sun-dried tomato butter on each one.

3 Place the husks back into original position to cover the corn. Using a string or a piece of the husks, tie the end of the corn so the butter stays intact.

4 Preheat a gas or barbecue grill.

5 Place the corn on the hot grill, approximately 425° F (220° C), and cook until tender. You will need to turn the corn every four to five minutes to get even cooking. This process will take approximately 20 minutes, depending on how hot your grill is.

To serve

Peel back the husks, making sure that some of the butter is still on the cob. Place on a platter or on individual plates.

Cornmeal Pudding
Polenta

SERVES 10–12

4	cups water
3³/₄	cups milk
1	tablespoon kosher salt
	Freshly-ground black pepper
3	cups polenta
2	tablespoons butter
¹/₂	cup grated Romano cheese
	Olive oil

TO PREPARE

1 In a large saucepan, add the water, milk and salt and pepper to taste. Bring to a boil over medium-high heat.

2 Lower the heat to medium. Using a heavy wooden spoon, stir in the polenta a little at a time, always stirring in the same direction. When all the polenta has been stirred in, the mixture should start to thicken.

3 Turn the heat down to medium-low and continue to stir vigorously and constantly in the same direction for about seven minutes.

4 Remove from the heat, add the butter and the Romano cheese, and blend thoroughly.

5 Lightly coat a work surface with the olive oil. Pour the polenta onto a large work surface, such as a 12-inch (30 cm) round wood board or an area on your counter top. Spread the polenta evenly to ¹/₂-inch (1.5 cm) thick and let cool completely to set up, about 30 minutes.

To serve

Cut the polenta into rectangular shapes about 2 x 3 inches (5 x 8 cm) and serve on a platter. You may also serve right away while it's still hot by simply spooning the polenta into a large bowl or serving platter.

We have a version of this recipe in our restaurant Pesce. –Johnny

We call it Creamy Chevre Polenta. You just add ¹/₂ cup of chevre (goat cheese) and 2 tablespoons of heavy cream in place of the Romano cheese. –Damian

The chevre puts a kick in it all right. It's got a nice little bite to it. –Johnny

Or for a richer polenta, try stirring in ¹/₃ cup of mascarpone cheese along with the butter and Romano cheese. Polenta is just good anytime, any which way. –Damian

Cornbread
Pane di Mais

SERVES 6–8

1 cup all-purpose flour
1 cup yellow cornmeal
$^1/_4$ teaspoon salt
1 tablespoon sugar
2 teaspoons baking powder
1 cup milk, or $^1/_2$ cup milk and $^1/_2$ cup sour cream
2 eggs
10 tablespoons butter, melted

TO PREPARE

1 Preheat the oven to 400° F (200° C). Place butter in a 10-inch (25 cm) cast iron skillet and place skillet in the oven.

2 Meanwhile, in a bowl mix together the flour, cornmeal, salt, sugar and baking powder.

3 In another bowl whisk together the milk (or milk and sour cream) and eggs.

4 Stir the wet ingredients into the dry ingredients until they are just mixed together. Do not overmix.

5 Remove skillet from the oven. Tilt and swirl melted butter in the pan to coat the sides then pour melted butter into the batter and stir to blend. Pour batter into the skillet and bake for 20 minutes, until done in the center and lightly golden on top. Test the center by sticking a toothpick in and removing quickly. If done, the toothpick will come out clean.

To serve

Cut into six to eight pieces and serve hot with softened butter and honey or jam.

We'd always eat cornbread with those good Sicilian meals of fried chicken and black-eyed peas. –Damian

That was our menu every New Year's Day. The black-eyed peas were for good luck. –Johnny

And the cornbread just went great with it. Boy, I love cornbread. –Damian

Cornbread Dressing
Ripieno di Pane di Mais

SERVES 6–8

1	recipe Giblet Stock, with chopped giblets and turkey neck meat (see page 168)
2	tablespoons butter
1	cup yellow onion, peeled and cut into medium dice
1	cup celery, cut into medium dice
1/2	cup red bell peppers, cut into medium dice
1/2	cup yellow bell peppers, cut into medium dice
1/2	cup green bell peppers cut into medium dice
1	double recipe Cornbread (see page 69), two days old, crumbled
2	cups white bread, two days old, cut into 1-inch (2.5 cm) cubes
1	bunch green onions, sliced
2	eggs
1	teaspoon chili powder
1/2	stick butter cut into small pieces for dotting
	Kosher salt and freshly-ground black pepper

TO PREPARE

1 Preheat the oven to 325° F (170° C).

2 In a large sauté pan, melt the butter on medium-high heat and add the onion, celery and peppers. Turn the heat down to medium and cook until soft, about 10 to 15 minutes. Remove from stove and let cool to room temperature.

3 In a large mixing bowl, add the cooked vegetables, corn bread and white bread. Add the chopped giblets, turkey neck meat, salt and pepper to taste.

4 Then add giblet stock to moisten the mixture to your liking; this will depend on the dryness of the cornbread. If you find you need more stock to moisten your dressing, you can simply add chicken stock or water.

5 Add the remaining ingredients to the bowl and mix well. Adjust seasoning.

6 Place in a greased casserole, dot with butter, cover with foil and bake for 40 minutes. Take the foil off and bake for an additional 15 minutes.

To serve

Excellent with any poultry or other white meat entrée.

NOTE: Giblets and turkey necks can be found prepackaged in the grocery meat department. If you can't find any prepackaged, request some from the butcher at the meat counter.

This dressing is for the holiday turkey. But if Mamma wasn't cooking for too many people, she used the same recipe to stuff hens. The chili powder stays way in the background, so it's real good going down. –Damian

Big D, you've never met a cornbread dressing you didn't like. –Johnny

Jalapeño Hushpuppies

SERVES 6

4 cups Canola oil for deep frying (approximate amount—more or less may be needed)

1 1/2 cups yellow cornmeal

1/2 cup all-purpose flour

1 teaspoon baking powder

1 teaspoon kosher salt

1 teaspoon Crystal hot sauce, or your favorite brand of hot sauce

1/4 cup minced green onions

1/2 cup cooked, crumbled bacon

1 tablespoon bacon drippings

2 jalapeños, seeded and minced

2 eggs, beaten

1/2 cup buttermilk

TO PREPARE

1 Preheat the Canola oil in a medium to large pan to about 350° F (180° C). You need at least three to four inches (8–10 cm) of oil in the pan.

2 In a large bowl, mix together the cornmeal, flour, baking powder, salt, hot sauce, onions, bacon and jalapeños.

3 Stir in the bacon drippings, eggs and milk. Mix until fully incorporated. If batter is too dry add a little buttermilk, a tablespoon at a time.

4 Drop a tablespoonful of the dough into the hot oil—you should be able to cook a maximum of four at a time. Fry the hushpuppies for two to three minutes or until they are golden brown. Stir and turn constantly to ensure overall browning.

5 Remove from the oil and drain on a paper-towel-lined plate.

To serve

Place the hushpuppies on a platter while hot and serve with your favorite tartar sauce—or for home-made Tartar Sauce, try our recipe (see page 172).

"Hush, puppy!" That's where they say the name came from—people tossing little bits of fried dough to their dogs to quiet them down. –Johnny

It's a Southern thing. –Damian

Except with the jalapeños and hot sauce. Then it becomes a Texas thing. –Johnny

Hushpuppies are great in place of french fries and onion rings too! –Damian

Uncle Manuel Mangiameli

Entrées
Piatti Forti

Around our family, entrées could be seafood or meat with equal ease. And either was just about as likely to turn up with the Italian sausage our family has made for generations. These photos are all about that wonderful sausage, which we use in our restaurants to this day. One shows Little Rocco Joseph Thomas with Big Rocco, learning how to make sausage from his Grandpa. The other shows the busy hands of Uncle Manuel Mangiameli, another rock-solid maker of terrific sausage.

One of the keys to entrées in our family is that they don't have to be huge. Sure, we all have pretty big appetites, but in a meal with appetizers, soup or salad, and of course pasta, you don't need a main course that'll kill you. Of course, we do eat portions that are large sometimes, and most of us end up living to be very old.

Little Rocco Joseph Thomas
with his Grandpa shown in background.

〜 Mamma's Pork Pot Roast

Mamma's Pork Pot Roast
Stracotto alla Mamma

SERVES 6–8

1	3—4-pound (1.4—1.8 kg) bone-in pork shoulder
8	large garlic cloves, peeled and cut into thick slices
24—30	Italian parsley leaves
	Kosher salt and freshly-ground black pepper
2—3	tablespoons vegetable oil
	All-purpose flour
1	carrot, peeled and coarsely chopped
1	celery rib, coarsely chopped
1	small yellow onion, peeled and coarsely chopped
4	large garlic cloves, peeled and coarsely chopped
2	cups boiling water
1/2	cup Italian parsley leaves

TO PREPARE

1 Preheat the oven to 325° F (170° C).

2 Pierce meat all over with a paring knife. Insert a piece of garlic and a few parsley leaves into the pierce marks.

3 Season meat very well with salt and pepper, rubbing seasoning into the meat evenly. Let seasoned meat sit for 30 minutes.

4 Heat the oil in a large roasting pan over medium-high heat. Meanwhile, flour the meat all over. Add the meat to the pan and brown on all sides, being careful not to scorch it.

5 About halfway through the browning process, add the carrot, celery, onion and coarsely-chopped garlic and let the vegetables brown a little.

6 When the vegetables and meat are brown, add the water and the parsley to the pan and cover. Place the pan in the oven and roast for three to four hours, turning the meat every hour until tender.

7 Remove roast from oven. Remove cover and let roast cool for about an hour.

8 Heat gravy and strain to remove vegetables.

9 This roast is best if made the day before. Slice cold and arrange in a 9 x 13-inch (23 x 33 cm) baking pan. Remove the hardened fat from the gravy while it's still cold.

10 Spoon the de-fatted gravy over the roast, cover with foil and heat in a 325° F (170° C) oven until warm.

To serve

Arrange the roast on a serving platter and pour the gravy over the top.

You know, Big D, if I was going to ask Grandma to make me just one thing, I think this would be it. –Johnny

It's real simple but real delicious. And it's even better the next day, sliced up and piled on Mamma's homemade bread. Kids in the third grade would always try to trade their mamma's peanut butter and jelly for my mamma's pork roast sandwich. –Damian

Mamma's Italian Meatloaf
Polpettone alla Mamma

SERVES 4–6

1/4	cup olive oil
1/2	red bell pepper, chopped medium
1/2	green bell pepper, chopped medium
1/2	yellow onion, peeled and chopped medium
1/2	bunch green onions, sliced
1	garlic clove, peeled and chopped fine
2	eggs
1	cup canned crushed tomatoes with juice
1	cup grated Pecorino Romano cheese
1	cup unseasoned breadcrumbs
1 1/2	teaspoons kosher salt
1	teaspoon freshly-ground black pepper
2	tablespoons chopped Italian parsley
2	pounds (900 g) ground beef
1	cup Mamma's Pomodoro "Tomato Sauce" (see page 173)

TO PREPARE

1 Preheat the oven to 400° F (200° C).

2 In a small sauté pan, heat the olive oil over medium heat and add the bell peppers and yellow onion. Cook, stirring occasionally, for about five minutes or until vegetables are soft.

3 Add the green onions and garlic and cook one minute more. Set the vegetables aside to cool.

4 In a mixing bowl combine the remaining ingredients except sauce. Add the cooled vegetables and mix well. Form into a loaf and place in a casserole dish just big enough to hold the meatloaf.

5 Place the meatloaf in the oven and cook for 15 to 20 minutes, or until nice and brown.

6 Pour the tomato sauce over the meatloaf, cover with foil, reduce the temperature to 350° F (180° C) and bake another 30 to 45 minutes, or until a thermometer inserted in the middle reads 150° to 160° F (66°–71° C).

7 Remove from the oven and let rest for 15 to 30 minutes.

To serve

Cut the meatloaf into slices about 3/4-inch (2 cm) thick and spoon some of the sauce from the pan over each slice.

NOTE: Instead of using 2 pounds of ground beef, you can use 1 pound of ground beef and 1 pound of ground pork.

Instead of gravy, Mamma always made her meatloaf with a tomato base in the sauce. –Damian

We like meatloaf with rice, lots of sauce from the meat loaf and mixed salad. –Johnny

Stuffed Peppers with Rice
Peperoni Ripieni Con Riso

SERVES 6

MEAT INGREDIENTS

1/2	pound (225 g) lean ground beef
1/2	pound (225 g) ground pork
1	yellow onion, peeled and finely diced
2	stalks celery, finely diced
2	tablespoons minced garlic
1	tablespoon chile flakes
2	teaspoons kosher salt
2	teaspoons freshly-ground black pepper
1/2	cup chopped fresh Italian parsley
2	tablespoons chopped fresh sage
1/2	cup walnuts, coarsely chopped

RICE INGREDIENTS

3	tablespoons butter
1/2	yellow onion, peeled and finely diced
1 1/2	cups arborio rice
3 1/2	cups store-bought or homemade Chicken Stock (see page 166), heated
1/2	cup grated Pecorino Romano cheese

PEPPER INGREDIENTS

6	blanched and peeled bell peppers, red, yellow, or green (see page 181)
1	recipe Mamma's Pomodoro "Tomato Sauce" (see page 173), heated

TO PREPARE THE MEAT

1 In a large skillet on medium heat, brown the beef and pork.

2 Add the onion, celery, garlic and the chile flakes and cook for five minutes. Season with the salt and pepper. Add the parsley, sage and walnuts. Mix well, remove from the heat and let cool.

TO PREPARE THE RICE

1 In a large saucepan, melt 1 tablespoon of the butter over medium heat and cook the onion in the butter for about three to four minutes until softened. Add the rice and stir well to coat the kernels with the butter.

2 Gradually add the warmed chicken stock about 1/2 cup at a time, adjusting the flame so you have a strong simmer and stirring constantly. When the rice has absorbed the stock, add another 1/2 cup. Continue this process until the rice is al dente, about 20 minutes.

3 Remove the pot from the stove and stir in the remaining butter and the grated cheese. Let cool.

4 Stir together the meat and the rice. Set aside.

TO PREPARE THE PEPPERS

1 Preheat the oven to 375° F (190° C).

2 Cut off the tops and stems of the peppers and remove the seeds. Keep the peppers whole without any holes or rips.

3 Spoon the meat and rice mixture into the peppers. Fill them to the top, but don't pack too firmly. Arrange open-end-up into a lightly-greased 9 x 13-inch (23 x 33 cm) casserole dish. Bake for 20 to 30 minutes or until the peppers are warmed through.

To serve

Pour Mamma's Pomodoro "Tomato Sauce" (see page 173) over the peppers in the casserole dish and serve.

Everybody's mamma or grandmama had a stuffed pepper recipe, but ours always had an Italian flavor to it. —Damian

In the old days, I'm sure they cut the filling with rice because meat was so expensive. Now we can afford meat, but we still love the rice. Our tastes work like that sometimes. —Johnny

Stuffed Rolled Beef
Braciole

SERVES 4–6

STUFFING INGREDIENTS

1	tablespoon butter
1/2	pound (225 g) chard leaves, de-stemmed and chopped
1/4	teaspoon kosher salt
1/4	teaspoon freshly-ground pepper
1/2	cup diced red bell pepper, 1/4-inch dice
1/2	cup toasted pine nuts
1/4	cup golden raisins
1	cup Mamma's Breadcrumbs (see page 171)
1	egg
1/4	cup Gorgonzola cheese, crumbled

MEAT INGREDIENTS

2 1/2 pounds (1.2 kg) round steak, tenderized and flattened to 1/4-inch (6 mm) thick

Olive oil

Kosher salt and freshly-ground black pepper

1 cup medium-bodied red wine

1–2 cups store-bought or homemade Beef Stock (see page 166), heated

Here's our variation on one of the great food traditions from Sicily, a dish that's on a million Italian-American menus. –Damian

In this recipe we use Mamma's Breadcrumbs. Every Sicilian Mamma had to have her own breadcrumbs, too. You just must have them. –Johnny

TO PREPARE THE STUFFING

1 Melt the butter on medium-high heat in a large sauté pan. Cook the chard for four to five minutes, until soft.

2 Add the salt, black pepper, red bell pepper, pine nuts and raisins and continue to cook for another two minutes.

3 Remove from the heat and let cool. Then add the breadcrumbs, egg and Gorgonzola cheese. Mix well and set aside.

TO PREPARE MEAT

1 Roll out the tenderized steak on a cutting board and brush with the olive oil. You can have your butcher tenderize the steak and then you can flatten it further with a mallet at home.

2 Season with a little salt and pepper to taste and spread the filling on the meat evenly. Leave a one-inch (2.5 cm) margin around the entire edge of the steak. Roll the steak up like a jelly roll and tie the meat at the ends and at one-inch intervals with a string to secure.

3 Preheat the oven to 350° F (180° C).

4 In a 12-inch (30 cm) cast iron or ovenproof skillet, pour in the olive oil just to cover the bottom of the pan and heat until almost smoking, about two minutes.

5 Add the rolled meat and brown on all sides. Add the wine and enough hot beef stock to come up to about $1/2$ inch (1.5 cm) in the skillet.

6 Cover the skillet with a lid or foil and place in the oven. Cook the steak for $2^{1}/_{2}$ hours, basting every 30 minutes. When it's done, remove the meat from the skillet and let it rest for 15 minutes.

7 Pour the pan juices into a gravy fat separator. Leave them for five minutes to let the fat float to the top. Carefully pour the de-fatted juices back into the pan.

8 Bring the juices to a boil and reduce the volume by one third. Season with salt and pepper if needed.

To serve

Remove the strings from the meat and cut into slices $1/2$-inch (1.5 cm) thick. Arrange on a platter and spoon the reduced pan juices over the top.

Or this beef roll can be dropped in Mamma's Sunday Sugo (see page 120) for the last two hours of cooking. Just brown on all sides and drop into the simmering sauce. When done, remove from sauce, remove string, slice and place on a platter with a little sauce.

It's great served with or after pasta.

Mamma's Sicilian Beef Stew
Spezzateddu alla Mamma

SERVES 6–8

¹/₄ cup vegetable oil
2¹/₂ pounds (1.2 kg) beef chuck, cut into 2-inch (5 cm) cubes
   Kosher salt and freshly-ground black pepper
   All-purpose flour for dredging
1 medium yellow onion, peeled and diced small
1 large green bell pepper, cut into 1-inch (2.5 cm) strips (optional)
4 cloves garlic, peeled and minced
2 cups of water
2 cups of store-bought or homemade Beef Stock (see page 166)
3 medium Yukon Gold or Yellow Finn potatoes, diced large
3 green onions, trimmed and sliced
2 cups finely-chopped Italian parsley
   Fresh parsley sprigs for garnish

TO PREPARE

1 Heat the vegetable oil on high in a large stew pot. Season the beef with salt and pepper to taste then dredge in flour (shake off excess) and brown meat in two batches. Remove the browned beef and drain on a paper-towel-lined plate.

2 Return meat to pot and add the onions to the browned beef and continue cooking on medium-high heat. Sauté onions until slightly soft, about five minutes. Add the peppers (if using) and garlic and continue to cook for another three minutes.

3 Add the water. Turn up the heat to high and reduce by one third, about five minutes.

4 Add the beef stock and potatoes and bring back to a boil. Turn the heat down to low and simmer for one hour, or until meat is fork-tender.

5 Stir in green onions and Italian parsley. Adjust seasoning.

Here's a real simple light gravy stew. Of course, you can always jazz it up a bit. –Damian

We'd always eat this when the year's first cold front blew in—though I guess in Houston, we should call them "cool fronts." –Johnny

To serve

Ladle the stew into large individual serving bowls and garnish with the parsley sprigs.

NOTE: If you want to jazz the dish up, you can replace the water with 2 cups of Chianti or medium-bodied red wine. Also, you can replace the green pepper with a red or yellow pepper.

Steak Braised in Chianti
Brasato al Chianti

SERVES 4–6

DRY RUB INGREDIENTS

1/2	teaspoon dried oregano
1/2	teaspoon dried thyme
1	teaspoon kosher salt
1/2	teaspoon freshly-ground black pepper

STEAK INGREDIENTS

2 pounds (900 g) bottom round, tenderized about 1-inch (2.5 cm) thick

1/2 ounce (15 g) or 1/2 cup dried porcini mushrooms, soaked in 1 cup boiling water for 30 minutes, drained and roughly chopped

3 tablespoons olive oil

3 cups peeled and sliced yellow onions

1/2 large red bell pepper, sliced 1/2-inch thick

1/2 large green bell pepper, sliced 1/2-inch thick

1/2 pound (225 g) crimini mushrooms, sliced 1/4-inch thick

2 tablespoons garlic, peeled and minced

1/4 cup grappa

1 cup Chianti

1 cup store-bought or homemade Beef Stock (see page 168)

2 bay leaves

2 sprigs fresh thyme

2 sprigs rosemary

Kosher salt and freshly-ground black pepper

Chopped fresh Italian parsley, for garnish

TO PREPARE

1 First, tenderize the bottom round by pounding it with a mallet until it is one-inch (2.5 cm) thick.

2 Mix the dry rub ingredients together. Rub all over the meat. Set aside.

3 Preheat oven to 350° F (180° C).

4 In a large cast iron or ovenproof skillet, heat the oil over medium-high heat until it sizzles, about two minutes. Sear the steaks two to three minutes on each side. Remove from the skillet and set aside.

5 Add the onions to the skillet and reduce the heat to medium. Cook for five minutes until they start to brown. Add the bell peppers and continue to cook for another minute.

6 Add the chopped porcini, crimini and garlic to the skillet and cook for two to three minutes, stirring often.

7 Add the grappa and scrape up any browned bits from the pan. Add the Chianti, stock, bay leaves, thyme, rosemary and salt and pepper to taste.

8 Return the steaks to the skillet, cover and bring back to a simmer. Place in the oven and cook for two to three hours or until fork tender.

9 Transfer the steak to a plate and cover with foil. Skim some of the fat from the surface of the gravy. Reduce the liquid on medium-high heat until thick.

To serve
Spoon some of the sauce over the steak and garnish with the parsley.

Everybody knows how these kinds of recipes get started: Someone is trying to make use of a cheaper cut of meat and they end up creating something wonderful. –Damian

I like this dish. It cooks a long time and makes a real nice sauce for dipping your bread in. –Johnny

Johnny C's Sausage

Johnny C's Sausage
Salsiccia

SERVES 10, OR MAKES 20 4-OUNCE (115 G) LINKS

1/4	cup salt
2	tablespoons freshly-ground black pepper
2	tablespoons red pepper flakes
1/3	cup fennel seeds
1	tablespoon granulated garlic
4	pounds (1.8 kg) ground pork (preferably from trimmed pork butt)
1	pound (450 g) ground beef (preferably from lean sirloin)
10	feet of pork casings (if frozen thaw under cold running water)
2	tablespoons vegetable oil or olive oil (to pan-fry sausage)

Oh, my dad makes this great sausage. My great-grandmother Bessie Palazzo gave the recipe to my dad, who had a grocery store and was a butcher. I can remember as a kid making this with my dad in the store. –Johnny

It's just one of those real special recipes. –Damian

If you don't want to make sausage links, you can use the same ingredients and form them into patties and pan-fry them instead. –Johnny

〜 *Left to right:* Johnny C. Carrabba, Jr., Johnny C. Carrabba, Sr. and Joe Carrabba.

TO PREPARE THE MEAT

1 In a bowl, mix all the spices together.

2 In another large bowl, combine the meat with the mixed spices until thoroughly incorporated. Cover and refrigerate for at least 24 hours so all the flavors will absorb into the meat.

3 To prepare the pork casing, pull about two to three feet at a time and wash under lukewarm water. Fit the end of the casing to the opening of the faucet and allow tepid water to run through the inside.

4 Then let the casing soak in cold water for 10 minutes. Drain and squeeze the water out. The casings are now ready for stuffing.

TO STUFF THE CASINGS

1 Use a large pastry bag and a large plain tube with at least a one-inch (2.5 cm) opening. Fill the bag about 2/3 full with the meat mixture and gather the casing by bunching it up against the tapered end of the piping bag.

2 Squeeze the meat into the casing and, every six inches (15 cm), twist the sausage to form links. When finished, tie up the ends and cut off any excess casing.

[Continued]

PIATTI FORTI

TO STUFF THE CASINGS
USING AN ELECTRIC GRINDER/STUFFER

1 Screw the stuffing funnel attachment into place. Gather the casing by bunching it up against the base of the funnel, leaving a small piece hanging so air can be "pushed" out of the casing.

2 If air pockets form in the sausage, you will find when you cut it there are "holes" in the meat and the meat will be gray.

3 Start filling the casing, lightly holding it at the base of the stuffer so that it does not unroll too fast as the meat comes out.

4 Every six inches (15 cm), twist the sausage to form the links and when finished, tie up the ends and cut off any excess casing.

TO COOK THE SAUSAGE

1 Prick each link a few times with a fork so they won't explode during cooking.

2 Place them in a large sauté pan, pour in enough water to come a quarter way up the sides of the links. Bring to a boil over medium-high heat, cover, reduce flame to low and steam for 10 minutes.

3 Remove the lid and let the water evaporate, about two minutes.

4 Once the water has evaporated, add the oil and cook the sausages about three minutes on each side until nicely brown. If your pan is not large enough, you may need to cook them in two batches.

These sausages are excellent served with our Peperonata (see page 48) and Polenta (see page 68). Place the polenta on a large serving dish or platter. Spoon the peperonata over the polenta and finish by arranging the sausages on top.

NOTE: Pork casings are mostly found in frozen blocks from your butcher or meat counter. Thaw them well under cold running water before using. The maximum casing length you can normally use on an electric grinder/stuffer is about two to three feet (60–90 cm) at a time.

Tamales

SERVES 10–12

DOUGH INGREDIENTS

4–5 large acorn squash

2   pounds (900 g) butter, softened

1 1/4 tablespoons baking powder

1   tablespoon salt

1 3/4 cups whole milk

7   cups masa harina

1 1/2 cups canned green chilies

2 1/2 cups grated Monterey jack cheese

MEAT FILLING INGREDIENTS

1/2 cup flour

1   teaspoon garlic powder

1   teaspoon onion powder

1   teaspoon black pepper

1   tablespoon chile powder

2   teaspoons salt

1   tablespoon cayenne pepper

1 1/2 pounds (750 g) stew meat also called chuck roast,
     cut into 1-inch (2.5 cm) pieces

2   tablespoons olive oil

1   dried red chile pepper

1   white onion, peeled and cut into small dice

1   green bell pepper, cut into small dice

1   14 1/2 ounce (415 g) can stewed tomatoes

1/2 cup almonds, coarsely chopped

2   tablespoons capers

1/2 cup golden raisins

8   green olives, pitted and coarsely chopped

1   tablespoon minced garlic

2   cups water

ADDITIONAL TAMALE INGREDIENTS

2   8-ounce (225 g) packages of dried corn husks,
     soaked in warm water for at least 2 hours or 1 pound
     (450 g) package frozen banana leaves, thawed

1   recipe Salsa Verde (see page 174)

     Butcher string, 12 yards

So why are we doing a Mexican dish on *Cucina Amore?* –Damian

Well, we grew up in Texas, right? A melting pot, right? And this is one of the best things that melting pot ever turned out. –Johnny

Now don't be afraid when you look at this recipe. You can do some of the steps in advance. The filling and the dough can be done up to a week ahead and kept in the refrigerator or in the freezer for up to a month. –Damian

[Continued]

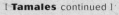
PIATTI FORTI

TO PREPARE THE DOUGH

1 Preheat the oven to 400° F (200° C).

2 Split the squash in half and scoop the seeds out. Place on a baking sheet and cook in the oven until soft, about 35 to 45 minutes. Scoop out the squash when it's cooled enough to handle.

3 In a small bowl, cream the butter with the baking powder and salt until it is light and fluffy and almost doubles in volume. Set aside.

4 In a small saucepan on medium heat, heat the milk until steaming but not boiling. Remove from the heat and pour into a food processor along with the roasted squash. Purée until smooth.

5 Transfer the purée to a bowl and mix with the masa harina. Stir in the butter mixture, add the chilies and cheese and refrigerate the mixture overnight until it sets up.

TO PREPARE THE FILLING

1 Preheat the oven to 375° F (190° C).

2 In a shallow bowl, mix together the flour, garlic powder, onion powder, chile powder, black pepper, salt and half the cayenne. Add the stew meat and coat well, shaking off any excess flour.

3 In a large ovenproof skillet, heat the olive oil on high and brown the meat on all sides in a single layer. You may need to do this in two batches to brown it properly.

4 Once all the meat is browned, add the dried chile to the skillet and cook for 20 seconds. Add the onion and bell pepper, stir and cook for two minutes.

5 Add remaining ingredients and the water, and cook on top of the stove for 20 minutes.

6 Place the skillet uncovered in the oven for one hour. Stir with a spoon occasionally to break the meat apart. You will want most of the liquid to evaporate and the meat to fall apart easily.

In Texas we use corn husks when making our tamales. –Johnny

But we've also included a method for using banana leaves. –Damian

Banana leaves? –Johnny

Well, you know we just have to add a few extra touches. –Damian

Naturally. –Johnny

TO ASSEMBLE THE TAMALES USING CORN HUSKS

1 Set up a collapsible vegetable steamer in a large deep saucepan with at least one inch (2.5 cm) of water in the bottom.

2 Line the steamer with some corn husk scraps to protect the tamales from direct contact with the steam and to add more flavor. Make sure to leave a few tiny spaces between the husks so condensing steam can drain off.

3 Keep the steamer on low while assembling the tamales and make sure to check the level of the water.

4 Cut four dozen 8- to 10-inch (20–25 cm) pieces of string or narrow strips of corn husk. Lay out a corn husk with the tapering end toward you.

5 Spread about 1/4 cup of the dough into about a 4-inch (10 cm) square, leaving at least a 1¹/2-inch (4 cm) border at the end toward you and a 3/4-inch (2 cm) border along the other sides.

6 Spoon about 1¹/2 tablespoons of the meat filling down the center of the dough.

7 Pick up the two sides of the corn husk and bring them together, causing the dough to surround the filling.

8 If the uncovered edges of the two long sides you're holding are narrow, tuck one side under the other; if wide, roll both sides over in the same direction around the tamale.

9 Fold up the empty 1¹/₂-inch (4 cm) section of the husk to form a tightly-closed bottom leaving the top open. Secure it in place by loosely tying one of the strings or a strip of husk around the tamale.

TO COOK THE TAMALES

1 As the tamales are being made, stand them on the folded bottoms in the prepared steamer. If you don't have enough tamales to fill the entire steamer, place loosely-wadded aluminum foil in the open spaces to keep the tamales from falling over.

2 Or you can stack the tamales in the prepared steamer. Do not stack them in the steamer more

TO ASSEMBLE THE TAMALES USING BANANA LEAVES

1 Set up a collapsible vegetable steamer in a large deep saucepan with at least 1 inch (2.5 cm) of water in the bottom.

2 Unfold the leaves and cut off the long hard sides where they were attached to the central vein. Check for holes or rips, then cut across the leaves with the grain to form unbroken 12-inch (30 cm) segments (you will need 36). Reserve the scraps.

3 Place the banana leaves in a steamer by loosely folding and stacking them. Steam the segments for 20 minutes to make them soft and pliable. They are now ready for assembling the tamales.

4 At this point it is also best to line the steamer rack with the reserved banana leaf scraps to protect the tamales from direct contact with the steam and to add more flavor. Make sure to

leave tiny spaces between the leaves so condensing steam can drain off.

5 Keep the steamer on low while assembling the tamales and make sure to check the level of the water.

6 Cut 36 12-inch (30 cm) pieces of string or thin strips of banana leaves.

7 One at a time, form the tamales: lay out a banana leaf segment, shiny-side-up, and spread ¹/₃ cup of the dough into an 8 x 4-inch (20 x 10 cm) rectangle on top of it.

8 Spoon 2 tablespoons of the filling over the left side of the rectangle of dough.

9 Then fold over the right third of the leaf so that the dough encloses the filling. Fold over the uncovered third of the leaf.

10 Then fold over the top and bottom. Loosely tie the tamales with string.

[Continued]

PIATTI FORTI

than two layers high, otherwise they will steam unevenly.

3 Don't tie the tamales too tightly or pack them too closely in the steamer, as they will expand when cooking. When all the tamales are in the steamer, cover them with a layer of leftover corn husks or banana leaf scraps.

4 Set the lid in place and steam over a constant medium heat for about 1¼ hours.

5 Watch carefully to make sure that all the water doesn't boil away and to keep the steam steady. Pour boiling water into the pot when more is necessary.

6 The tamales are done when the leaves peel away from the masa easily. Let the tamales stand in the steamer off the heat for a few minutes to firm up.

7 For the best texture, let them cool completely. Then steam again for about 15 minutes to heat them through.

To serve

Untie the banana leaves or corn husks, remove the tamale and serve with Salsa Verde.

NOTE: If you want to keep assembled, fully-cooked tamales in the freezer, they will keep for up to four to six months in a resealable freezer bag and then wrapped in foil. To reheat, simply thaw them in the refrigerator overnight and then cook in a steamer for 20 minutes until hot.

Banana leaves can be found at grocery stores specializing in Asian foods and corn husks can be found at grocery stores specializing in Mexican and Latin foods.

Left to right, friends Louis Marino, Sam Covernale, Damian's dad Paw Paw Mandola and Nick LaGate.

Barbecue Pork Spare Ribs

SERVES 4–6

1   recipe Spice Rub (see page 175)
6   pounds (2.7 kg) baby back pork ribs (about 3 whole racks), cut into four to six rib sections
1/2 cup beer (for oven method)
1   recipe Tony "Nino" Mandola's Barbecue Sauce (see page 172)

TO PREPARE USING A BARBECUE PIT

1 Rub the spice mixture over both sides of the ribs. Let ribs marinate in the refrigerator for two hours.

2 Light the wood or charcoal in the firebox of the pit. When white ashes are present place marinated ribs in the smoke-box of the pit. Maintain 250° F (130° C) throughout the cooking time (see page 186). Cook ribs for about one hour, turn ribs over and cook another hour.

3 Wrap ribs in foil and cook another 30 minutes.

To serve

You can either leave the rib sections whole, depending on how many people you are serving, or you can cut between the bones into individual ribs. Transfer to a platter and serve while still hot with Tony "Nino" Mandola's Barbecue Sauce, warmed, on the side.

TO PREPARE USING OVEN METHOD

1 Preheat the oven to 300° F (150° C).

2 Rub the spice mixture over both sides of the ribs. Arrange the ribs on a large baking sheet. Pour in the beer, cover with foil and bake for three hours. Once out of the oven let the ribs cool slightly before grilling.

3 Using smoking wood chips, have your barbecue grill reach a medium heat or if using a gas grill, heat to medium-high heat, also using the wood chips.

4 Arrange the ribs on the barbecue or gas grill and cook until they are nicely caramelized and crispy on the edges, occasionally turning them with tongs.

You've got some options when you're shopping for ribs. You can buy a whole rack, of course. But sometimes baby backs are sold in sections of four to six, in case you don't want to cook too many. –Damian

But we always want to cook too many. And you can get a headstart on this recipe a day in advance by rubbing the ribs with the spices and refrigerating them on a baking sheet. –Johnny

Barbecue Beef Brisket

SERVES 8–10

1   5–6-pound (2.25–2.7 kg) beef brisket, fat cap left on
1   recipe Spice Rub (see page 175)
$^1/_2$ cup beer (for oven method)
2–3 cups Tony "Nino" Mandola's Barbecue Sauce (see page 172)

The best thing about this brisket is the beer. Paw Paw Mandola was a great barbecuer, and he'd always make his brisket with beer. Not cooking it with beer, but drinking beer while he cooked it! –Johnny

My dad would put already cold beer in the freezer for about 10 minutes and serve it in an old Army tin cup. –Damian

We were just kids, but he'd always give us a slice of this brisket and a sip of that icy beer. –Johnny

Other than the essential beer it's important that you use good smoky chips, such as hickory, or maybe pecan or oak. We'd never heard of mesquite back when we were growing up. Maybe somebody in Texas had some, but not anybody at our house. –Damian

TO PREPARE

Coat the brisket with the Spice Rub on both sides. Place in a baking dish and marinate for two hours in the refrigerator.

TO PREPARE USING A BARBECUE PIT

1   Light wood or charcoal in the firebox of the pit. When white ashes are present place marinated brisket in the smoke-box of the pit, fat cap down. Maintain 250° F (130° C) throughout the cooking time (see page 184).
2   Cook brisket for about two hours, turn brisket over with the fat cap on top and cook another two hours. Turn meat with tongs or heavy rubber gloves. Never puncture meat with a fork.
3   Wrap brisket in foil and cook another two hours.

To serve

Trim off fat cap. Slice the brisket as thick or thin as you want, carved against the grain. Arrange on a platter and serve with Tony "Nino" Mandola's Barbecue Sauce, warmed, on the side.

ENTRÉES

TO PREPARE USING OVEN METHOD

If you don't have a barbecue pit you can still get pretty good results with an oven or an oven and a grill.

1   Preheat the oven to 300° F (150° C).
2   Place brisket in a large baking dish. Pour the beer into the baking dish, cover with foil and bake for 3½ to 4 hours. Check periodically to make sure there is still liquid in the bottom of the dish. If necessary, add more beer or water.

3   Remove from the oven and place brisket on a hot grill and sear on both sides to get some smoky flavor, transfer the brisket to a cutting board and let it cool slightly. Or you can skip the grill and just bake the brisket—you will not have that smoked taste.
4   While the brisket is cooling, pour the drippings into a gravy separator and wait five minutes for the fat to come to the top.
5   Place the barbecue sauce into a medium saucepan and carefully pour the de-fatted drippings into the sauce, stirring well. Turn the heat to medium high and bring the sauce just to a simmer. Remove from the heat and set aside.

⌒ *Top:* Cousin John Carrabba from Dallas with John C. Carrabba and John C. Carrabba Jr. looking out of the truck window.

⌒ *Right:* Grandpa and Grandma Testa in front of their grocery in Houston.

91

Grilled T-Bone Steak with Herbed Garlic Sauce

Grilled T-Bone Steak
with Herbed Garlic Sauce
Bistecca alla Fiorentina e Ammoghiu

SERVES 6. MAKES ABOUT ONE QUART (1 L) OF SAUCE

SAUCE INGREDIENTS

1/4 cup peeled garlic cloves

1 1/2 teaspoons salt

3/4 teaspoon freshly-ground black pepper

1/2 cup fresh basil leaves

1/3 cup fresh mint leaves

1/4 teaspoon dried oregano

1/4 cup freshly-squeezed lemon juice

2 tablespoons white wine vinegar

3/4 cup extra-virgin olive oil

STEAK INGREDIENTS

3 t-bone or rib-eye steaks about 1-inch (2.5 cm) thick

Olive oil

Kosher salt and freshly-ground black pepper

1 recipe of Johnny C's Grill Baste (see page 174)

TO PREPARE THE SAUCE

1 Place the garlic, salt, pepper, basil leaves, mint leaves and oregano in a mortar and pulverize with a pestle until you have a paste.

2 Place the paste in a glass jar and add the lemon juice, vinegar and olive oil. Refrigerate. Before using, bring to room temperature and shake well. This sauce will hold in the refrigerator for two weeks.

TO PREPARE THE STEAK

1 Preheat a gas or charcoal grill or your oven broiler.

2 If using a gas grill, lightly coat the steak with olive oil on both sides, season with salt and pepper to taste and place on a hot grill.

3 Baste the steak with Johnny C's Grill Baste to flavor the meat while cooking.

4 Cook about four to six minutes per side, making crisscross marks from the grill on the meat by turning it over halfway through the cooking and laying back on the grill in the opposite direction. (The four to six minutes time should give a medium-rare temperature.) For a rarer steak, cook about a minute less on each side, and for a well-done one, about two minutes more on each side.

5 If using a broiler, put the steak on a baking sheet, season with salt and pepper and place on the top rack under the broiler. Follow the same directions for cooking times above.

To serve

Let the steaks rest for five minutes after removing them from the grill—this will let the juices remain in the steaks. Place on a platter or single plates with Potato Celeriac Gratin (see page 58). Pass the Ammoghiu.

This recipe makes it on our list of our Top Five Favorite Meals of All Time. –Johnny

Johnny, your Top Five list seems to have about a thousand things on it! –Damian

It's good to have a list, Big D. But you really shouldn't limit yourself. –Johnny

Okay, so we won't. This Ammoghiu sauce is great not just on steak but on broiled chicken as well. Man, it even works on fried chicken. And some of our customers even dip their bread in it. –Damian

Shrimp, Chicken and Andouille Jambalaya

SERVES 10–12

1/4	cup extra-virgin olive oil
2	cups finely-chopped yellow onion
1	cup finely-chopped celery
1	cup finely-chopped green bell pepper
2	tablespoons Big D's Bayou Blend (see page 175)
8	cloves garlic, peeled and chopped
1	pound (450 g) andouille sausage, cut into 1/4-inch (6 mm) slices
1	pound (450 g) boneless white and dark chicken meat, cut into 1-inch (2.5 cm) cubes
1	pound (450 g) medium shrimp, peeled and de-veined
3	cups medium grain uncooked rice
2	cups canned crushed tomatoes
4	cups Shrimp Stock (see page 167)
2	tablespoons Crystal Hot Sauce, or your favorite hot sauce
2	tablespoons Worcestershire Sauce
1/4	teaspoon cayenne pepper
2	teaspoons kosher salt
1/2	teaspoon freshly-ground black pepper
1	cup sliced green onions

TO PREPARE

1 Heat the olive oil in a large Dutch oven over medium heat. Add the onion, celery, peppers and 1 tablespoon of Big D's Bayou Blend. Cook, stirring often, for about 15 minutes or until the vegetables are browned.

2 Add the garlic and cook for one minute. Add the sausage and cook for 5 to 10 minutes.

3 Season the chicken and shrimp with the remaining tablespoon of Big D's Bayou Blend. Add the chicken to the pot and cook for 10 minutes. Then add the shrimp and cook for two more minutes.

4 Remove shrimp. Add the rice and stir two to three minutes. Add the remaining ingredients except for the green onions and bring to a boil. Stir well, cover and reduce the heat to a simmer.

5 Cook for 15 to 17 minutes until the rice is tender and the liquid is absorbed. Remove from the heat and let rest, covered, for 10 minutes. Stir in the green onions and serve.

To serve
Spoon on plates and serve with your favorite green salad and a tall glass of beer or iced tea.

My grandmama had a Louisiana background, so we had the best of all worlds—Italian, Creole and Cajun. –Johnny

Mamma made jambalaya quite a bit. This is our own spin on the dish. –Damian

Shrimp Creole
Gamberi alla Creole

SERVES 6

1 1/2	pounds (750 g) shelled medium shrimp
2	teaspoons Big D's Bayou Blend (see page 175)
1/2	cup extra-virgin olive oil
1	cup chopped onions, medium
1	cup chopped celery, medium
1/2	cup chopped bell peppers, medium
4	cloves garlic, peeled and chopped fine
5	tablespoons tomato paste
1	cup tomato purée
3	cups water
1	teaspoon sugar
1/4	teaspoon cayenne pepper
	Kosher salt and freshly-ground black pepper
1	cup sliced green onion
1	cup chopped fresh Italian parsley
1	recipe White Rice (see page 177)

TO PREPARE

1 Lay the shrimp out on a large plate and season with 1 teaspoon of Big D's Bayou Blend and set aside.

2 In a large heavy pot, heat the olive oil over medium heat and add the onion, celery and bell peppers and cook until soft, about five minutes. Add the garlic and cook one more minute.

3 Add the tomato paste and cook, stirring for three minutes. Add the tomato purée, water, sugar, the remaining Big D's Bayou Blend, cayenne, salt and pepper to taste and bring to a boil. Reduce the heat to low, cover, and simmer for 30 to 45 minutes.

4 Add the shrimp, green onion, and parsley and cook five minutes more.

To serve

Adjust the seasoning to taste and ladle the Shrimp Creole over White Rice in individual serving bowls.

This recipe is from our executive chef at *Pesce*, Mark Holley, who is a great Creole cook. –Damian

Yeah, he's from Dayton, Ohio but was "Creolized" by the *Brennan's* family when he was at *Brennan's* in Houston. –Johnny

You see J. C., even a Yankee can be taught to cook Cajun! –Damian

Damian's Gumbo

SERVES 8–10

ROUX INGREDIENTS
3/4 cup vegetable oil
1 1/2 cups all-purpose flour

GUMBO INGREDIENTS
1 cup chopped yellow onions, medium
1/2 cup chopped green onions, medium
1 cup chopped celery, medium
1/2 red bell pepper, chopped medium
1/2 green bell pepper, chopped medium
1/2 cup fresh Italian parsley, chopped fine
3 large garlic cloves, peeled and chopped fine
2 cups crushed canned tomatoes
2 tablespoons gumbo filé (ground sassafras)
2 teaspoons freshly-ground black pepper

1/2 teaspoon cayenne pepper
1 tablespoon Big D's Bayou Blend or your favorite Cajun spice powder
1/2 tablespoon dried oregano
3 bay leaves
1 tablespoon Tabasco Sauce, or your favorite hot sauce
1/2 tablespoon Worcestershire Sauce
1 gallon Shrimp or Fish Stock (see page 167), heated up
3/4 pounds (350 g) okra, trimmed and sliced 1/2-inch (1.5 cm) thick
1/2 dozen cleaned crabs with claws
1 1/2 pounds (750 g) medium shrimp, peeled and deveined
1 pound (450 g) jumbo lump crab meat
1 recipe White Rice (see page 177)

When it comes to gumbo, anybody's gumbo, I think the roux is the most important part, because it not only thickens the dish but at the same time gives it so much flavor and color. –Damian

How about the stock? –Johnny

That, too. But the gumbo has to have a little texture to it, and it's got to be dark. And that's what the roux does. –Damian

TO PREPARE THE ROUX

Add the oil to a large stockpot over low heat. Then gradually add flour, stirring constantly, until smooth and you have a very dark roux (see page 184). Do not burn.

TO PREPARE THE GUMBO

1 Add the yellow onions, green onions, celery, bell peppers and parsley to the roux and cook until soft.
2 Add the garlic, tomatoes and filé and cook two minutes more. Add the spices, Tabasco Sauce and Worcestershire Sauce and stir to incorporate. Stir in the hot stock, okra and crabs and bring to a boil.
3 After the gumbo has come to a boil, reduce the heat to a strong simmer and cook for one hour. Add the shrimp and crab meat to the pot 15 minutes before serving.

To serve

Ladle into bowls, each with a half cup of white rice in the bottom. Serve with Mamma's Bread (see page 170) and enjoy.

Shrimp Étouffée
Gamberi Étouffée

SERVES 4–6

SAUCE INGREDIENTS

4	tablespoons all-purpose flour
2	tablespoons vegetable oil
	Sauce Ingredients
4	cups Shrimp Stock (see page 167)
1	tablespoon Crystal Hot Sauce or your favorite brand of hot sauce
1	tablespoon Worcestershire Sauce
1	tablespoon Big D's Bayou Blend (see page 175)
4	bay leaves
1	teaspoon kosher salt

SHRIMP INGREDIENTS

8	tablespoons butter
1	cup sliced yellow onion
1/2	cup red bell pepper, julienned 1/4-inch
1/2	cup green bell pepper, julienned 1/4-inch
1/2	cup finely-chopped celery
2	tablespoons finely-chopped garlic
2	pounds medium shrimp, peeled, deveined, tails left on
2	tablespoons Big D's Bayou Blend (see page 175)
1/2	cup white wine
1/4	cup chiffonade of green onions
1	recipe White Rice (see page 177)

TO PREPARE THE ROUX AND SAUCE

1 In a small saucepan, stir together the flour and oil over low heat. Slowly cook the flour and oil to a dark brown color (see page 184), being careful not to burn it. Set the roux aside.

2 In another saucepan, add the shrimp stock, Hot Sauce, Worcestershire Sauce, Big D's Bayou Blend, bay leaves and kosher salt. Bring to a boil over medium-high heat.

3 With a whisk, add the roux a little at a time until it is completely incorporated. Reduce the heat to low and simmer for five minutes. Remove the sauce from the heat. Strain through a wire mesh sieve and set aside.

TO PREPARE THE SHRIMP

1 Melt the butter in a large sauté pan over medium heat. Cook the onion, bell peppers and celery until soft and golden, about 10 minutes. Add the garlic and cook one minute more.

2 Spread the shrimp out onto a large platter and season with Big D's Bayou Blend. Add to the sauté pan and cook for two minutes, then pour in the wine, continue cooking for one minute.

3 Add the strained sauce and simmer for four minutes. Remove from the heat and stir in the green onions.

To serve

Spoon this mixture over White Rice either in bowls or on plates, and accompany it with a green salad.

Damian of course thinks his Bayou Blend seasoning is the big key to this dish. But I disagree. I think there's a whole lot more going on than that. –Johnny

It's really a great recipe. The roux gives it a nutty flavor. Plus, it's got a little kick thanks to the seasoning, Johnny. It's traditionally served over white rice. But it's also terrific over pasta or even polenta. –Damian

When something's this good it goes with anything! –Johnny

Creole Shrimp and Crab Boil

Creole Shrimp and Crab Boil
Lesso di Gamberi e Granciporri alla Creole

SERVES 6–8

8	quarts water
$^1/_2$	cup Crystal Hot Sauce, or your favorite brand of hot sauce
$^1/_2$	cup Worcestershire Sauce
2	cups coarsely-chopped celery
2	cups peeled and coarsely-chopped carrots
2	cups coarsely-chopped yellow onions
$^1/_2$	cup peeled whole garlic cloves
$1^1/_2$	cups Zatarain's Liquid Crab Boil, or substitute another brand in liquid form or in a dry spice packet
$^1/_2$	cup whole black peppercorns
4	lemons, cut in half
$^1/_2$	cup Big D's Bayou Blend or your favorite Creole spice mix
$^1/_2$	cup cayenne pepper
8	whole bay leaves
2	cups kosher salt
5	pounds (2.25 kg) shrimp, shells left on
	Cubes of ice from one ice tray
5	pounds (2.25 kg) fresh, lively blue crabs

TO PREPARE

1 Combine all ingredients except the shrimp, crabs and ice cubes in a large stockpot or kettle. Bring the mixture to a boil over high heat, then reduce the heat and simmer for five minutes.

2 Remove half of the liquid to a large bowl and put in the ice cubes to cool the mixture down. Set aside.

3 Bring the remaining half of the mixture back to a boil and add the shrimp. Cook for one to three minutes, depending on the size and amount of the shrimp.

4 When the shrimp are cooked, remove them from the mixture and quickly submerge them in the chilled liquid for at least 10 minutes. Repeat the process with the crabs. Crabs will take about five to eight minutes to cook.

To serve

Drain the liquid off and serve the boil on a large platter. We spread plenty of newspaper on the table for the discarded shrimp and crab shells and to make sure the seasoning doesn't stain the table. No sauce is required, due to the wonderful flavor from the boiling liquid. You could add a Cocktail Sauce however, if you choose (see page 172). Enjoy!

To have a good shrimp or crab boil, you really need to season your water well. –Damian

You always need a lot more seasoning than you think you need, because most of it stays in the water. –Johnny

Mamma's Whole Roasted Fish
Pesce Arrosto alla Mamma

SERVES 4

PIATTI FORTI

1	4-pound (1.8 kg) whole fish, such as snapper, red fish or sea bass, de-scaled, gills and fins removed, (see page 182)
3	tablespoons extra-virgin olive oil
	Kosher salt and freshly-ground black pepper
3	cloves garlic, peeled and roughly chopped
2	sprigs parsley
2	sprigs oregano + 1 tablespoon, chopped
1	lemon, sliced into very thin rounds
1/2	cup sliced green onion
1	cup crushed canned tomatoes with juice
	Fresh parsley sprigs for garnish
	Lemon wedges for garnish

TO PREPARE

1 Preheat the oven to 400° F (200° C).

2 Follow method for cleaning fish (see page 182) or have your fishmonger do it for you.

3 Pour some olive oil into a large roasting dish, just enough to coat the bottom. Score the fish along the body in two or three places on both sides. Lay the fish in the dish and pour a little more olive oil over it. Season the fish with salt and pepper inside and out, making sure to get the seasoning inside the slits. Rub the chopped garlic in the slits and inside the cavity. Place the sprigs of parsley and oregano inside the cavity.

4 Lay the slices of lemon on top and sprinkle over the green onions, tomato, chopped oregano and salt and pepper to taste. Drizzle with a little more olive oil.

5 Bake for about 30 minutes until the flesh is white and flaky.

To serve

Present the whole fish on a platter and garnish with parsley and lemon wedges.

We'd always eat this around the Feast of St. Joseph, which as every good Sicilian knows is March 19. –Damian

It's a big Sicilian feast day. –Johnny

Except it's a feast with no meat, because it's during Lent. With this roasted fish on the table, we had no trouble feasting anyway. –Damian

Salt Cod with Stewed Tomatoes and Onions
Baccalaru Cefalutana

SERVES 4

2	pounds (900 g) Baccalaru (salt cod)
1/4	cup extra-virgin olive oil
1	small yellow onion, peeled and diced small
2	cloves garlic, peeled and sliced
1/2	cup white wine
2	cups canned crushed tomatoes
1	pound (450 g) potatoes, cut into 1-inch (2.5 cm) cubes
1	teaspoon red pepper flakes
	Kosher salt and freshly-ground black pepper to taste (watch the salt since the cod is also salted)
2	teaspoons chopped fresh Italian parsley
2	teaspoons chopped fresh oregano
1	cup pitted Sicilian green olives

TO PREPARE

1 Soak the salt cod in cold water for 24 hours, changing the water several times. This will take most of the saltiness out of the fish. Drain the salt cod and pat dry. Cut into approximately four-ounce (115 g) pieces.

2 Heat the olive oil in a saucepan over medium heat. Add the onion and cook until soft and starting to caramelize, about two minutes. Add garlic and cook one minute. Add the white wine and cook off the alcohol, about one minute.

3 Add the tomatoes, potatoes, red pepper, salt and freshly-ground black pepper to taste, cover and cook until potatoes are almost done, about five to seven minutes.

4 Add the salt cod, parsley, oregano, and olives and cover again. Cook for about 10 minutes and serve.

To serve

We would serve this in shallow bowls. It's a one-pot dish; all you need on the side is a salad.

This dish is named after Cefalú in Sicily, the hometown of my grandmother and grandfather Testa. It's a beautiful little town, right down the coast from Palermo. They salted the cod so they'd always have fish year round, even when they had none fresh. Now we have lots of fresh cod, but Sicilians still love the taste of this dish.
–Damian

At our house, we always had this dish, or some variation on it, on Christmas Eve.
–Johnny

That shows you just how special it is. –Damian

Mamma's Oyster Loaf

Mamma's Oyster Loaf
Panino di Ostriche Fritti alla Mamma

SERVES 4

3	cups vegetable oil for deep frying, add more if needed
16	medium size oysters, shucked, oyster liquid reserved (see page 182)
	All-purpose flour for dredging
1	cup cornmeal
1¹/₄	teaspoons salt
³/₄	teaspoon freshly-ground black pepper
¹/₄	teaspoon cayenne pepper
1	tablespoon Big D's Bayou Blend (see page 175)

1	loaf of Mamma's Bread (see page 170) or a store-bought 6–7-inch (15–18 cm) round Italian bread

OPTIONAL TOPPINGS

¹/₄	cup Cocktail Sauce (see page 172)
8	peperoncini, julienned
1	bunch celery hearts with leaves, washed and roughly chopped
12	Sicilian green olives, pitted and chopped

TO PREPARE

1 In a heavy two-quart (2 l) saucepan, preheat the vegetable oil to 350° F (180° C). You need at least 1¹/₂ inches (4 cm) of oil in the saucepan.

2 In a bowl, stir together the cornmeal, salt, pepper and cayenne pepper. Dip each oyster in the reserved oyster liquid or water. Dredge oyster in flour and dip back into the oyster liquid or water. Coat the oysters in the seasoned cornmeal and shake off the excess.

3 Put only eight of the oysters in the hot oil at a time and cook them until golden brown and just cooked through, no more than 1¹/₂ minutes.

4 Transfer to a paper-towel-lined plate. While they are still hot, sprinkle on the Big D's Bayou Blend if you wish to use it. Repeat this process with the remaining eight oysters.

5 Cut the bread round in half horizontally. Hollow it out a little by removing some of the inside of both the bottom and top halves. On both halves of the bread, spread as much of the cocktail sauce as you wish to use.

6 Arrange the oysters on the bottom half of the bread and top with peperoncini, celery and green olives. Put the top half back on. Press down firmly to adhere all the ingredients together.

To serve

Cut the sandwich into at least four wedges and serve immediately. It is great with our Italian Potato Salad (see page 27).

What can I say? I think this was the best thing we ever made on our TV show! –Johnny

We like to do it Sicilian-style. –Damian

My grandmother used to scoop the inside out of the bread. So we didn't eat too much bread—and so we could really taste what was inside. –Johnny

And that scooping, they did that over in New Orleans, too. They called the sandwich an oyster loaf. And the old Creoles who got their wives mad at them always brought home an oyster loaf, and then I guess they kissed and made up and made babies. –Damian

Hmm... I never knew a sandwich could do that. –Johnny

Well, it's got to be a real good sandwich. –Damian

Gulf Coast Fried Seafood
Fritto Misto di Pesci al Gulf Coast

SERVES 6

3³/4 cups cornmeal

1   cup corn flour

2   tablespoons kosher salt

1¹/4 tablespoons freshly-ground black pepper

4–5 pounds (1.8–2.2 kg) assorted fish fillets such as
speckled trout, catfish, red fish, oysters, shrimp;
cut the fish into 2- or 3-inch (5 or 8 cm) wide pieces

1   batch Big D's Bayou Blend (see page 175)

1–2 cups Crystal Hot Sauce or Louisiana Hot Sauce
Vegetable oil for deep frying

1   batch Cocktail Sauce for dipping (see page 172)

1   batch Tartar Sauce for dipping (see page 172)

1–2 lemons cut into wedges

TO PREPARE

1 In a large pan, preheat the vegetable oil to 350°
to 360° F (180°–185° C). You will need about 4 to 5
inches (10–13 cm) of oil.

2 For the breading, mix the cornmeal, flour, salt
and pepper in a large bowl. Pour out onto a shallow bowl, large plate or platter. Set aside.

3 Lay the seafood out on a large platter, lightly
season it with Big D's Bayou Blend and let sit for
10 minutes. Reserve any leftover seasoning for
later use.

4 Pour the hot sauce into a large bowl. Dip the
seafood into the hot sauce and then the cornmeal
breading to coat well. In the large pan with the
preheated oil, fry a few pieces of fish at a time
until each is a light golden brown.

5 Drain on a paper-towel-lined platter. To keep
warm, you can put into a 225° F (110° C) oven
until you are done frying all the fish.

To serve

Arrange the fish on a large platter. Garnish with
lemon wedges for squeezing on the fish right
before eating. Cocktail and Tartar Sauces both
accompany the fish nicely. Fries and Coleslaw go
well with this dish, too (see pages 62 and 38).

This is what we cook when Damian
and I go fishing. –Johnny

You always want to fry fish the same
day you catch it. And it's always good
with a little avocado salad. And a lot
of French fries. –Damian

And a cold beer. –Johnny

And good tartar sauce. –Damian

Fried Chicken
Pollo Fritto

SERVES 4

SEASONING DUST INGREDIENTS
1   tablespoon dried oregano
1   tablespoon dried basil
1   teaspoon cayenne pepper
1   teaspoon freshly-ground black pepper

CHICKEN INGREDIENTS
6   cups all-purpose flour
1/2   cup salt
1/2   cup freshly-ground black pepper
2   tablespoons granulated garlic
1   tablespoon onion powder
1   teaspoon cayenne pepper
1   3-pound (1.4 kg) fryer chicken, cut up, washed and left wet
    Vegetable oil for frying chicken

TO PREPARE THE SEASONING DUST

Grind the oregano, basil, cayenne pepper and black pepper in a spice grinder or blender, to a powder consistency. This can be stored in an air-tight container until needed.

When we started working on our TV series, the producers asked us our favorite meal. They asked us separately, like they were on some cop show and wanted to trip us up. And, both Damian and I said fried chicken. –Johnny

Nobody does great fried chicken anymore. –Damian

This recipe just might change that! –Johnny

We've jazzed ours up with a seasoning dust. –Damian

There you go getting cute on us again! –Johnny

TO PREPARE THE CHICKEN

1 Place all the remaining dry ingredients in a large grocery bag and shake well.
2 Place the chicken pieces in the same bag and shake well. Place the whole bag in the refrigerator and let the chicken sit in the flour mixture for one hour, re-shaking every 15 minutes.
3 In a large cast iron skillet, preheat about 2 inches (5 cm) of vegetable oil to 350° F (180° C) until it starts to sizzle. Cook the chicken pieces on all sides until golden brown. Remove the chicken and place on a paper-towel-lined plate. Sprinkle with the seasoning dust and let cool about 15 minutes before serving.

To serve

As our go-to-heaven meal we would serve this Fried Chicken with mashed potatoes and butter peas.

ENTRÉES

Brick Chicken
Pollo al Mattone

SERVES 4–6

2 whole chickens, (each about 2¹/₂ pounds (1.2 kg)
 Kosher salt and freshly-ground black pepper
7 tablespoons extra-virgin olive oil
2 tablespoons rosemary, coarsely chopped
¹/₂ cup sliced garlic, slivered
¹/₂ cup store-bought or homemade Chicken Stock (see page 166)
1 lemon, juiced
¹/₄ cup sherry vinegar
2 tablespoons butter
2 tablespoons chopped fresh Italian parsley
 Extra herbs for garnish

In Italy, this one's called Pollo al Mattone, meaning chicken under a brick. The Italians have a terra cotta top for cooking the chicken instead of actually using a brick. By pressing down on the chicken, you get the skin crispy while keeping the meat juicy, because you're cooking it in half the time. –Damian

It's a good idea to use small chickens, because they cook faster. –Johnny

TO PREPARE

1 Preheat the oven to 400° F (200° C).

2 Cut each chicken in half and remove the back-bones—or you can totally de-bone the chicken if you prefer. Lay plastic wrap on the counter, put the chicken halves on top and cover with another sheet of plastic. Pound and flatten each chicken half so they are all uniform in thickness. Season both sides with salt and pepper.

3 Heat 2 tablespoons of the olive oil in each of two cast iron or ovenproof skillets on medium high until it starts smoking.

4 Place 2 chicken halves in each pan, skin-side-down, and put a heavy weight on top, such as a few bricks that have been wrapped in foil or a cast iron pan. Press firmly to flatten the chicken further. Adjust heat so that chicken cooks at a lively pace but doesn't burn. Cook for eight to ten minutes.

5 Then place the pans in the oven with the weights still on to finish cooking for an additional 15 to 20 minutes. Once the chickens are cooked, take it out of the pans and set aside on a platter.

TO PREPARE THE SAUCE

1 Put one of the pans back on the stove top on medium heat and add the remaining 3 tablespoons of olive oil. Add the rosemary and garlic and stir quickly for about 30 seconds while they toast in the oil.

2 Pour in the chicken stock, lemon juice and sherry vinegar. Remove the pan from the stove, swirl in the butter and mix well.

To serve

Place chicken on individual plates or platter. Drizzle the sauce over the top of the chicken and garnish with coarsely-chopped Italian parsley. This chicken is great served with our Potato Dumplings (Gnocchi) (see page 127).

NOTE: Chicken can be served with sauce, lemon wedges or as is.

Johnny C's Grilled Chicken
Pollo alla Griglia

SERVES 4–6

2   3-pound (1.4 kg) fryer chickens, cut into breasts, legs, thighs and wings
     Kosher salt and freshly-ground black pepper
1   recipe Johnny C's Grill Baste (see page 174)

My dad bought an Old Smoky grill and there was a recipe in it for grilled chicken.

–Johnny

He took that recipe and doctored it up.

–Damian

All my cousins love my dad's grilled chicken. He cooks it real slow, so it stays real juicy. That's the main thing. You never want it to get all dried out. –Johnny

Another way to cook it is on a rotisserie instead of the grill. My brother Vincent makes a great spit-roasted chicken at his restaurant, Vincent's, in Houston. –Damian

TO PREPARE

1   Preheat a gas or charcoal barbecue grill. Set the rack five to six inches (13–15 cm) above the heat.

2   Season the chicken with salt and pepper and place on the hot grill. With a brush, baste the chicken with the Grill Baste. Cook four to five minutes on each side for the breasts and six to seven minutes for the thighs and legs.

3   Turn all the pieces over a third time and cook an additional four to five minutes for the breasts and six to seven minutes for the thighs and legs. Baste well before and after every turn.

4   The chicken pieces should have an internal temperature of 165° F (74° C) and the juices in the thighs and legs should run clear. Make sure you baste the chicken throughout the cooking process.

To serve

Place the chicken on a platter and add a little more baste (without any raw chicken juices in it) on top. Any potato or vegetable recipe in this book will go with this chicken. If you prefer, you can serve the chicken with Tony "Nino" Mandola's Barbecue Sauce (see page 172).

NOTE: If there is any question about whether there are raw chicken juices in the baste, you can bring the baste to a boil and cook for three to five minutes. This will eliminate any health issues.

~ Mamma Grace and her sister-in-law, Aunt Margeret Mandola Lampasas cleaning chickens at Uncle Joe Mandola's farm in Tomball, Texas.

Roasted Turkey
Tacchino Arrosto

SERVES 6–8

BRINE INGREDIENTS

1	10- to 12-pound (4.2–5.4 kg) turkey
1 1/2	gallons of water
1 1/2	cups salt
1	cup sugar

INGREDIENTS

2	tablespoons fresh oregano, very coarsely chopped
2	tablespoons fresh thyme, very coarsely chopped
2	tablespoons fresh parsley, very coarsely chopped
5	cloves garlic, peeled and sliced
2	medium onions, peeled and cut into medium dice
2	carrots, peeled and cut into medium dice
2	celery stalks, cut into medium dice
3	tablespoons unsalted butter, softened
2	cups white wine
1/3	cup flour
1	recipe Giblet Stock (see page 168) and reserved turkey neck pieces
	Kosher salt and freshly-ground black pepper

For Thanksgiving we'd have roasted turkey, just like everybody else in America. –Damian

Yeah, but we'd have Italian dishes, too. –Johnny

We'd always "Italianize" everything, even Thanksgiving, with Italian main courses and side dishes. –Damian

For this recipe, we brine the turkey with a salt solution. This step adds flavor to the bird and makes the meat juicy. But you can omit this step if you prefer. –Johnny

TO BRINE THE TURKEY

1 Brine the turkey for 10 to 12 hours prior to cooking. To make the brine, line the bottom half of your turkey roaster with a small, plastic kitchen garbage bag. The edges will overlap, but you'll need these later. Now pour in the water, salt and sugar and mix thoroughly.

2 Place the turkey in the brine and loosely tie the top of the bag to keep the turkey covered and refrigerate. About midway through the brining process (five to six hours), untie the bag, turn the turkey over and cover, and refrigerate again for the remaining time.

TO ROAST THE TURKEY

1 Preheat the oven to 450° F (230° C). Remove the turkey from the brine and pat dry. Season the bird with pepper and salt inside the cavity and out.

[Continued]

2   Place half of the herbs inside the bird along with one of the onions, 1 carrot, 1 celery stalk, and 2 cloves of garlic. Place the rest of the vegetables in the roasting pan to make a base for the turkey.

3   In a bowl mix the remaining garlic with the remaining herbs.

4   Stuff the herb mixture underneath the skin by first taking the handle of a rubber spatula and running it underneath the skin to loosen. Then distribute the herb mixture evenly under the skin by using the handle of the rubber spatula.

5   Next, take the butter and rub on the outside of the turkey, coating it well. Set the bird on the vegetables and roast in the oven for 30 minutes.

6   Lower the temperature to 375° F (190° C) and cook 12 minutes per pound, approximately 2 to 2 1/2 hours. The internal temperature of the thighs should reach 165°–170° F (74°–77° C) and the juices should run clear.

7   After one hour of cooking, pour 1 cup of the wine in the roasting pan and baste the bird every 30 minutes to get a crispy skin.

8   Once the bird is done, remove it from the oven and transfer to a carving board. Loosely cover with foil and let it rest for 20 minutes before carving.

TO PREPARE THE GRAVY

1   While the turkey is resting, make the gravy by separating the turkey juices from the fat. Pour the juices into a gravy fat separator. Let the fat rise to the surface, which takes about five minutes.

2   While it is separating, put the roasting pan on the stove top on medium heat. Sprinkle in the flour and, with a wooden spoon, stir the flour around as you scrape up the turkey bits for about one to two minutes.

3   Using a whisk, stir in the remaining wine and reduce the volume by half, about one minute. Now stir in the de-fatted turkey juices along with the Giblet Stock.

4   Turn the heat up to medium-high and bring to a boil for about five to seven minutes until the gravy is thickened and the flour flavor is cooked out.

5   Stir in the reserved, chopped turkey neck pieces from the Giblet Stock, adjust for seasoning if needed and pour into a gravy boat.

TO CARVE THE TURKEY

1   Pull off each leg. Place the leg on a plate and separate the thigh from the drumstick at the joint. Slice the thigh around the bone. Slice the drumstick, arranging the dark meat on a hot plate.

2   With a long, thin knife, cut each of the breasts straight down into very thin slices, holding the turkey with a fork while cutting. Separate the wing at the joint and place with the dark meat.

To serve

For a Thanksgiving Dinner, place the turkey slices on a platter with the Cornbread Dressing (see page 70). Serve with Braised Fennel (see page 65) and Southern Baked Yams (see page 63). Pass around the gravy boat and enjoy! Then for dessert serve up some Lena Vallone's Pecan Pie (see page 156).

Breast of Pheasant Sautéed with Mushrooms

Fagiano Saltate con Funghi

SERVES 4

2	tablespoons olive oil
2	whole breasts of pheasant
3	tablespoons diced pancetta
1	tablespoon minced shallot
2	garlic cloves, peeled and sliced
10	crimini mushrooms, thinly sliced
	Kosher salt and freshly-ground black pepper to taste
1/2	cup Marsala
1	cup store-bought or homemade Chicken Stock (see page 166)
3	tablespoons butter
2	tablespoons coarsely-chopped Italian parsley

TO PREPARE

1 Preheat the oven to 400° F (200° C).

2 In an ovenproof pan that is large enough to fit the breasts, heat the olive oil on medium high until sizzling. Sear the breasts skin-side-down until browned, about two minutes, and repeat on the other side. Once the breasts are browned, place them in the oven for eight minutes. Remove from the oven, remove the breasts from the pan, and let them rest.

3 Meanwhile add the pancetta to the same pan and cook for about three to four minutes to render the fat. Add the shallots and garlic and cook until softened, approximately two minutes. Then add the mushrooms, stirring to coat the mushrooms well, and season with the salt and pepper.

4 Deglaze the pan with the Marsala and reduce the volume of the liquid by half. Add the stock and reduce again by half the volume.

5 Return the breasts to the pan and coat them with the sauce. Add the butter and parsley and cook for two more minutes, until the sauce comes together and the meat is cooked and heated through. Add more stock if needed to cook the breasts longer.

To serve

Place one breast half on each of four individual serving plates and spoon some of the sauce over the top. This is excellent served with Creamy Chevre Polenta (see page 68).

This is a great dish for fall and winter. Be sure to pick out a very lean bird. –Damian

The sweetness of the Marsala and those mushrooms go so well with pheasant. –Johnny

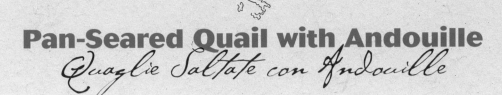

Pan-Seared Quail with Andouille
Quaglie Saltate con Andouille

SERVES 4

MINT BOURBON GLAZE INGREDIENTS

1/3 cup bourbon, such as Jack Daniels

1/3 cup water

1/3 cup sugar

1/3 cup mint leaves

QUAIL INGREDIENTS

8 quail

   Kosher salt and freshly-ground black pepper

2 tablespoons olive oil

SAUCE INGREDIENTS

1/2 cup small-diced onions

4 tablespoons seeded minced Serrano peppers (or substitute jalapeño peppers)

1 tablespoon minced garlic

1/2 cup andouille sausage, taken out of the casing

4 tablespoons bourbon, such as Jack Daniels or Jim Beam

1 1/4 cups store-bought or homemade Chicken Stock (see page 166)

   Kosher salt and freshly-ground black pepper

1/4 cup julienned mint

This recipe is from our sous chef at *Pesce*, Javier Lopez. We really like it with its garlic and Serrano pepper sauce and the mint bourbon glaze. –Damian

The glaze is my favorite. It's kind of like finishing off the quail with a mint julep.

–Johnny

TO PREPARE THE MINT BOURBON GLAZE

1 In a non-reactive saucepan (stainless or copper), mix together the bourbon, water and sugar. Bring to a boil on medium-high heat and reduce the volume by half, or until a syrupy consistency.

2 Remove from the heat, add the mint and let steep for 20 minutes. Strain out the mint and reserve sauce for later use. Set aside the glaze.

TO PREPARE THE QUAIL

1 Wash quail under cold water and trim the tips of the wings off with shears. Place them breast-down and, with the shears or a sharp knife, remove the backbone and discard. Cover with plastic wrap and gently pound the quail with a wooden mallet so they are slightly even.

2 Preheat the oven to 375° F (190° C).

ENTRÉES

Left to right: Charles Petronella, Nash D'Amico, Damian and Phillip Barletta in Damian's first restaurant, Huntsville, Texas, 1975

3 In a large ovenproof sauté pan, heat the olive oil until almost smoking, about three minutes. Season the quail with salt and pepper and place in the pan breast-side-down. Cook for four minutes or until lightly browned.

4 Turn the quail over and move the pan to the oven to cook for an additional four to five minutes. You will know the birds are cooked when clear juices flow. When finished cooking, transfer them to a platter and cover to keep warm.

FOR THE SAUCE

1 Put the sauté pan back on the stove top on medium heat and add the diced onions, serrano peppers and garlic and cook for two to three minutes.

2 Add the sausage, mash to break up, and cook for another two minutes. Pour in the bourbon, chicken stock and salt and pepper, and cook for two more minutes. Then add the julienned mint to the sauce.

To serve

Spoon the sauce over the quail on the platter. Then drizzle a little Mint Bourbon Glaze over the top of the quail and serve. This dish goes well with Creamy Chevre Polenta (see page 68) and any of your favorite vegetables.

Left to right: Sam Lampasas, Sam D. Mandola, Mary Lampasas, Hazel Roman Mandola, Lena Lamonte Mandola, Joe Mandola, Margaret Mandola Lampasas, Ciro Lampasas Sr., Frank Mandola, Frank Lamonte, Lucy Palazzo Mandola, Lou Lamonte, Tony A. Mandola Sr., Grace Testa Mandola, Frances Mandola Corona, Charles B. Corona

Pasta & Pizza

Pasta & Pizza

In some ways, we Carrabbas and Mandolas cooked a lot like other people along the Texas Gulf Coast, blending the fresh sea foods we found close at hand with the Creole and Cajun influences that sneaked across the Sabine River from Louisiana. But in some ways we were Sicilian through and through—our love affair with pasta and pizza being one of those ways.

You have to understand that just about any collection or combination of ingredients you like can be transformed into a pasta sauce, a pizza topping or both. That meant that when we were having pasta or pizza, we never had a clue what was about to show up on the table.

A great big plate of pasta comes to mind when we look at some of these photos—like the one showing Damian's parents with some of his aunts and uncles,

just one generation from Sicily, at the End of Main Club in Houston. There was no way to get this many members of our family in one place without promising them pasta. The other photo was shot on vacation in California in the 1940s.

Soaking up the California sun are Johnny's great grandparents, Bessie and John Palazzo, along with his grandfather, John Carrabba, Sr., holding his daughter Bessilynn, his father Johnny Carrabba, Jr. and his cousin Vita Ann Zarzana.

Clockwise from upper left:

Great Grandpa John C. Palazzo, Great Grandma Bessie Palazzo, Grandpa John C. Carrabba Sr., Bessilynn Carrabba Piazza, Dad Johnny C. Carrabba Jr., Vita Ann Zarzana Palermo

Pasta with Tomato and Garlic

Pasta with Tomatoes and Garlic
Pasta Sostanza

SERVES 4

1/2 cup extra-virgin olive oil

6 cloves garlic, peeled and medium chopped

1 28-ounce (790 g) can whole Italian tomatoes, chopped fine

1/2 pound (8 ounces) (225 g) angel hair pasta

Kosher salt and freshly-ground black pepper

1/2 cup grated Romano cheese

TO PREPARE

1 Heat olive oil and garlic in a large saucepan over medium-low heat. When garlic starts to brown, add the tomatoes with juice, and increase the heat to medium high.

2 Season with salt and pepper to taste. When the tomatoes start to boil, reduce the heat and simmer for 15 minutes.

3 Meanwhile, set a large pot of salted water to boil. When water comes to a boil, add the pasta and cook until very al dente–only about 1 1/2 minutes–pasta will finish cooking in the sauce.

4 Drain the pasta, reserving the water.

5 Add the pasta to the sauce and stir in enough of the reserved pasta water (about 1/2 to 1 cup) to make the consistency somewhat soupy. Turn the temperature back up to medium high, cook for one to two minutes so the pasta absorbs some of the liquid and finishes cooking.

To serve

Ladle into individual serving bowls. Pass the Romano cheese. (Grandpa Mandola would add a pat of butter to his.)

Sostanza means sustenance. Here's a quick dish my Grandmother Mandola liked to make. Sometimes those quick little pastas are the best. –Damian

Yeah, it's real quick—maybe a good choice for lunch or a Friday dinner. It's intended sure to make you feel good right away. –Johnny

Now that's what I call sostanza! –Damia

Spinach Lasagne with Meat Sauce
Lasagne Verdi

SERVES 8–10

MEAT SAUCE INGREDIENTS

2 tablespoons extra-virgin olive oil
$1/2$ cup sliced pancetta
$1/4$–$1/2$ cup finely-chopped onion
2 tablespoons finely-chopped carrot
2 tablespoons finely-chopped celery
1 pound (450 g) lean ground beef
1 pound (450 g) lean ground pork
  Kosher salt and freshly-ground black pepper
  A pinch of freshly-grated nutmeg
$3/4$ cup dry white wine
3 tablespoons tomato paste
$1 1/2$ cup water

SPINACH LASAGNE INGREDIENTS

$3 1/2$ cups all-purpose flour
2 tablespoons olive oil
$1/4$–$1/2$ cup cooked chopped spinach, squeezed dry
2 eggs

BÉCHAMEL SAUCE INGREDIENTS

6 tablespoons butter
1 cup all-purpose flour
1 quart (1 l) milk, heated to boiling
  Kosher salt and freshly-ground black pepper
  A pinch of freshly-grated nutmeg

ADDITIONAL INGREDIENTS

1 cup + 2 tablespoons freshly-grated Parmigiano Reggiano cheese
3 tablespoons butter

My grandmother would always cook us our favorite dish for our birthday. –Johnny

When we were kids, that meant lasagne. –Damian

She'd let us know how much work it was—but she'd do all the work with tender loving care. –Johnny

Of course, there are all kinds of lasagne. This is a great one with the spinach lasagne and béchamel sauce. You can add sautéed eggplant as a layer, too! –Damian

TO PREPARE THE MEAT SAUCE

1 Heat oil in a Dutch oven or large saucepan over medium heat. Add pancetta and cook until browned. Add onion, carrots, celery and continue cooking, stirring constantly with a wooden spoon, until browned.

2 Add beef, pork and salt and pepper to the same pan and dust lightly with nutmeg. Continue cooking, stirring constantly, until meat loses all pink color, about 30 minutes.

3 Reduce heat to medium-low. Add wine and continue cooking, stirring occasionally, until wine has evaporated (five to ten minutes). Blend in tomato paste.

4 Add water to cover all ingredients. Raise heat to medium-high and bring to boil. Then reduce heat and simmer uncovered about 45 minutes, stirring occasionally. Remove from heat.

TO PREPARE THE SPINACH PASTA

1 While the meat sauce is cooking, combine all ingredients for the lasagne noodles and knead until smooth. Roll out on lightly-floured surface to a thickness of about $1/8$ inch (or use pasta machine and roll quite thin). Cut into $5^{1}/_{2}$- to 6-inch (14.5–15 cm) squares, re-rolling scraps and cutting as many additional squares as possible.

2 Bring a large quantity of lightly-salted water to a boil in a large pot on high heat. Add half of the pasta and cook just until al dente, about one minute.

3 Place finished pasta in bowl of ice water to stop the cooking process and keep the pieces separated. Then drain the pasta well and lay flat on dish towels to dry.

4 Repeat steps 2 and 3 with remaining uncooked pasta.

TO PREPARE THE BÉCHAMEL SAUCE

1 Melt butter in a 3-quart (2.75 l) saucepan over medium heat. Whisk in flour, blending well. Whisking constantly, continue cooking for two minutes.

2 Slowly whisk in boiling milk, blending until smooth. Add salt and a pinch of nutmeg. Reduce heat to low and cook about 10 minutes, stirring constantly. Set aside.

TO ASSEMBLE

1 Preheat oven to 350° F (180° C). Generously butter a 9 x 13-inch baking dish. Spread a little of the béchamel sauce on the bottom of the baking dish so the pasta doesn't stick to it.

2 Arrange a layer of pasta in the bottom of the dish. Spread evenly to cover with about $1/3$ of the béchamel sauce and then some of the meat sauce. Sprinkle with about $1/3$ of the cheese.

3 Repeat layering. Finish with another layer of pasta, then remaining béchamel and cheese. Dot with butter. Bake until hot and bubbly, about 40 minutes.

4 Remove the lasagne from the oven and place on a wire rack to cool for about 30 minutes. The resting will let the lasagne firm up so it can be cut into squares and not be runny.

To serve

Serve with remaining meat sauce and additional Parmesan cheese on the side if desired.

Magnolia Macaroni Factory, Houston, Texas with delivery driver.

Pasta and Meatballs with Mamma's Sunday Gravy (Sugo)

Pasta e Polpette con Sugo di Pomodoro

MEATBALL INGREDIENTS

2	medium yellow onions, peeled and coarsely chopped
2	bunches green onions, coarsely chopped
2	garlic cloves, peeled
1/2	cup chopped fresh Italian parsley leaves
1 1/2	cups chopped fresh basil leaves
3	eggs
1	cup unseasoned breadcrumbs
1 3/4	cups water
3/4	pound (350 g) grated Romano cheese
4	tablespoons salt
1	teaspoon freshly-ground black pepper
3 1/2	pounds (1.6 kg) ground beef
3 1/2	pounds (1.6 kg) ground pork
	Olive oil for frying meatballs

MAMMA'S SUNDAY GRAVY (SUGO) INGREDIENTS

1	cup extra-virgin olive oil
2	medium yellow onions, chopped fine
10	medium cloves garlic, chopped fine
20	large basil leaves, chopped fine
5	6-ounce (175 g) cans tomato paste
2	28-ounce (790 g) cans crushed tomatoes
1	28-ounce (790 g) can tomato purée
15	cups water
	Salt and freshly-ground black pepper to taste
5	green onions, chopped fine
1	cup vegetable oil
2	pounds pork butt, picnic, or shoulder (bone in)
2	pounds chuck roast (bone in)
10	whole basil leaves
2	pounds (900 g) of your favorite pasta

We call this Meatballs with Sunday Gravy because it was the first part of your typical Sunday meal. There is usually some other meat like pork or beef in the sauce too but we always had to have the meatballs. –Damian

After the pasta, meatballs, meat and gravy, we'd have a roast, salad, vegetables. It was a ritual. –Johnny

TO PREPARE THE MEATBALLS

1 Place the onions, green onions, garlic, parsley and basil in a food processor and chop fine. Add eggs and blend a minute more.

2 Place the onion mixture in a bowl large enough to hold all the ingredients. Add the rest of the ingredients except the meat. Mix well, blending all the spices thoroughly. Add the meat and mix well.

3 Roll the mixture into two-inch (5 cm) wide balls, using warm water to keep your hands moist.

4 Heat enough oil to come up one inch (2.5 cm) in a large sauté pan to 350° F (180° C) degrees. Cook the meatballs on all sides until brown. Drain on paper towels. Or you can cook them, on a baking sheet in a preheated 375° F (190° C) oven for 12 to 15 minutes or until brown. Drain on paper towel.

TO PREPARE MAMMA'S SUNDAY GRAVY AND COMPLETE DISH

1 In a 12-quart (11.5 l) pot place the olive oil, onion, garlic and chopped basil over medium heat and cook, stirring occasionally, for eight to ten minutes, or until onions are soft and translucent.

2 Add tomato paste and cook for five minutes, stirring frequently to keep paste from burning. Add crushed tomato and purée and mix thoroughly to blend with paste. Rinse the tomato cans out with some of the water and add all of the water to the pot. Stir sauce well to mix in water and raise heat to bring sauce to a boil.

3   While sauce is coming to a boil prepare pork and chuck roast: Trim as much of the fat from around the outside of the meat as possible. Heat the vegetable oil in a large skillet over medium-high heat and when the oil is hot, add the meats one at a time and brown on all sides.

4   When sauce comes to a boil, reduce heat, let simmer for a few minutes, season with salt and pepper and then remove some of the sauce to be used for baked eggplant or other meatless dishes. Cool sauce you are not using immediately and store in the refrigerator in a plastic container with a tight fitting lid.

5   Transfer the pork and chuck roasts to the sauce and reduce the sauce to a simmer. Add the green onions then partially cover the pot and simmer the sauce for three hours, stirring occasionally so the sauce does not burn.

6   In the last hour of cooking, meatballs should be added to Mamma's Sunday Gravy (Sugo). Leave the top of the pot askew and finish cooking for the last hour.

7   When the sauce is done, adjust seasonings, add the remaining basil leaves to the top of the sauce and cover tightly. Let sauce sit for a few minutes and then remove the lid and stir in the basil that was sitting on top of the sauce.

8   Drop 2 pounds (900 g) of your favorite pasta in lightly-salted boiling water and boil until al dente.

To serve

Remove pork, beef and meatballs and place in a warm serving bowl on the table. Drain pasta and place in a warm serving platter. Ladle enough sauce onto the pasta to coat. Toss and ladle a little more sauce on top. Put some extra sauce in sauce boats and place on table. Put pasta on table. Place pasta on individual plates with some pork, beef and a couple of meatballs. Pass the sauce boat and grated Romano cheese and dig in.

NOTE: Eat as much as you want, but remember, this is just the first course! Everyone but the cooks should be at the table while the pasta is boiling and the last assembly is being done. Hot pasta waits for no one. As soon as the pasta hits the table it needs to be eaten piping hot!

Seafood Pasta

Seafood Pasta

Linguine Sole e Mare

SERVES 4

1/4	cup extra-virgin olive oil
6	ounces (175 g) medium shrimp (21/25 count), peeled to tail and de-veined
4	ounces (115 g) medium scallops
4	ounces (115 g) calamari, bodies and tentacles
4	cloves garlic, medium chopped
1/4	cup sun-dried tomatoes packed in olive oil (reserve 2 tablespoons of the oil), julienned
1/4	cup pitted Calamata olives, quartered lengthwise
1/2	cup fresh tomatoes, peeled, seeded and chopped
4	ounces (115 g) crab meat, cleaned of shell
1	pound (450 g) linguine
1	tablespoon butter, softened
1/4	cup torn fresh basil leaves
1/4	cup whole Italian parsley leaves, for garnish
	Kosher salt and freshly-ground black pepper

TO PREPARE

1 Heat olive oil in a large sauté pan over medium-high heat. Season shrimp and scallops with salt and pepper to taste and add to pan. Sauté for about two minutes. Season the calamari and add to pan along with the garlic and cook one minute longer.

2 Add sun-dried tomatoes, along with the 2 table-spoons of their reserved oil, then add the olives and the tomatoes and cook one minute. Add crab, being careful not to break large pieces. Taste and adjust seasoning.

3 Boil pasta in a large pot of salted water until al dente. Drain and transfer pasta to the seafood mixture. Toss, add the butter and basil and toss again.

To serve

Place the pasta in the center of a large serving platter. Arrange the seafood attractively on top. Sprinkle whole parsley leaves over dish and serve immediately.

I love pasta with seafood. This is the kind of pasta I was brought up on. –Damian

This dish has lots of sun in it, with sun-dried tomatoes and olives. –Johnny

Plus some pretty wonderful shrimp, scallops, calamari and crab meat. It's bound to please! –Damain

Tomato, Basil and Mozzarella Pizza
Pizza alla Margherita

MAKES ONE 10–12-INCH (25 TO 30 CM) PIZZA

1   recipe Pizza Dough (see page 171)
4   tablespoons extra-virgin olive oil
1   cup chopped fresh mozzarella
1/2 cup canned tomatoes, drained, seeded and crushed fine
     Kosher salt and freshly-ground black pepper
6–8 fresh basil leaves, torn in thirds

TO PREPARE

1 Preheat the oven to 500° F (260° C).

2 Place the oven rack on the lowest level in the oven. If using a pizza stone, place it on the rack in the oven and make sure it preheats for one hour before baking. If you are using a pizza pan, brush with a little olive oil before placing the pizza dough on the pan (see page 171).

3 To assemble, brush the top of the dough with the olive oil. Spread on the tomatoes to within 1/2 inch of the edge of the dough. Then sprinkle on the mozzarella and salt and pepper to taste.

4 If you are using a pizza stone, transfer the pizza to the oven. Bake between 12 to 14 minutes, or until the edges are golden brown.

5 If you are using a pan, place in the oven for 10 to 12 minutes and bake on the lowest rack until the edges are golden. Again, cook for longer if needed.

To serve

Remove the pizza from the oven and place on a cutting board. Drizzle over the remaining 2 table-spoons olive oil. Garnish with torn basil leaves by spreading them evenly on top, and let the pizza cool for five to ten minutes. Then cut and serve.

This is the classic pizza from Naples, that everybody loves. –Johnny

It's best if you use fresh mozzarella. –Damian

And be sure to use really good olive oil! You can taste the difference. –Johnny

Mushroom Pizza
Pizza con Funghi

MAKES ONE 10–12-INCH (25 TO 30 CM) PIZZA

1	recipe Pizza Dough (see page 171)
1/4	cup + 2 tablespoons olive oil
2	cups assorted wild mushrooms such as hedgehog, chanterelle, black trumpet, shiitake, morel, porcini, cleaned and cut in half
1/4	cup shredded smoked mozzarella
1	cup caramelized shallots or red onions (see page 182)
2	tablespoons chopped fresh thyme
	Kosher salt and freshly-ground black pepper

FOR THE MUSHROOMS

In a large skillet, heat 1/4 cup of olive oil on medium-high heat until almost smoking, about two minutes. Add the mushrooms and stir to coat well. Season with salt and pepper and cook for four to five minutes until the liquid has evaporated. Cool to at least room temperature before topping the pizza.

FOR THE PIZZA DOUGH AND TO ASSEMBLE

1 Preheat the oven to 500° F (260° C).

2 Place the oven rack on the lowest level in the oven. If using a pizza stone, place it on the rack in the oven and make sure it preheats for one hour before baking. If you are using a pizza pan, brush with a little olive oil before shaping the dough on the pan (see page 171).

3 To assemble, brush the top of the pizza dough with 2 tablespoons of olive oil. Sprinkle on the mozzarella, mushrooms, caramelized onions or shallots and the thyme. Finish with a sprinkling of salt and pepper to taste.

4 If you are using a pizza stone, transfer the pizza to the oven. Bake 10 to 12 minutes, longer if needed until the edges are golden brown.

5 If you are using a pan, place in the oven for 12 to 14 minutes and bake on the lowest rack until the edges are golden. Cook for longer if needed.

To serve

Remove pizza from the oven and place on a cutting board. Cool for five minutes before cutting and serving.

Smoking the mozzarella gives this pizza a real extra zip. –Damian

We love to serve this mushroom pizza in the wintertime. –Johnny

But, of course, there's no time of year that Johnny doesn't love mushrooms! –Damian

Sicilian-Style Pizza
Faccia di Vecchia (Sfinciuni)

SERVES 4–6

1	recipe Pizza Dough (see page 171)
8	tablespoons extra-virgin olive oil
1	cup small shards of Pecorino Romano cheese
12	sardines, de-boned and cut into small pieces (canned in olive oil)
12	anchovies, cut into small pieces (canned)
2	cups canned crushed tomatoes or 2 large ripe tomatoes, chopped
1	tablespoon roughly-chopped garlic
1 1/2	teaspoons chopped fresh oregano or 3/4 teaspoon dried
1/2	teaspoon kosher salt
	Liberal pinch crushed red pepper

TO PREPARE

1 Preheat the oven to 400° F (200° C).

2 Brush a 15 1/2 x 10 1/2-inch (39 x 26 cm) jelly roll pan with 2 tablespoons of the extra-virgin olive oil. Place the dough in the pan and using your hands, gently press and stretch it out to reach the sides. Brush the dough evenly with 2 more tablespoons of extra-virgin olive oil.

3 Distribute the ingredients in this order over the dough: 1/2 cup of the shards of Pecorino Romano cheese, sardines, anchovies. At this point, gently press the cheese, sardines and anchovies into the dough.

4 Continue layering with the tomatoes, garlic, oregano, salt, crushed red pepper and Pecorino Romano cheese. Drizzle the remaining extra-virgin olive oil all over the top.

5 Bake in the oven for approximately 30 minutes, rotating the pizza once so that it evenly browns.

To serve

Let the pizza cool five minutes then cut into squares and serve. It can be eaten warm or at room temperature.

The name means Face of an Old Woman, which sounds a bit weird. But it's a great Sicilian anchovy and sardine bread. We love it during the holidays! –Damian

My uncle Tony Mandola makes the best version I've ever tasted. But, this comes close. –Johnny

Potato Dumplings
Gnocchi di Patate

SERVES 6–8 AS AN ENTRÉE OR 10–12 AS AN APPETIZER. 10 DOZEN SMALL GNOCCHI

1   pound (450 g) russet potatoes
3/4 cup (115 g) all-purpose flour
2   egg yolks
1   tablespoon kosher salt
3–3 1/2 cups Gorgonzola Sauce (see page 173)

TO PREPARE

1   Preheat the oven to 350° F (180° C). Bake the potatoes for one hour or until completely cooked.
2   Peel the potatoes and press the flesh through a potato ricer. Place the hot riced potatoes in a mixing bowl.
3   Add the flour, egg yolks and salt to the potatoes and mix until dough just comes together. This process should be done quickly (15 to 30 seconds), as overworking the dough will make the gnocchi heavy and sticky.
4   Shape the dough into a ball. Pull off a section of the dough and roll it by hand on a lightly-floured surface into a long cylinder, about 1/2-inch (1.5 cm) thick. Cut into 1/2-inch (1.5 cm) pieces.
5   Then roll the pieces on a gnocchi paddle or over the back of a fork to create an oval shape with indentations. Continue with the remaining dough and place all the gnocchi on a lightly-floured tray until ready to cook.
6   Cook the gnocchi in a large pot of slow boiling, lightly-salted water. The gnocchi are done as soon as they float to the surface, about two minutes. Do this in three batches so as not to overcrowd the pot.
7   Have a large sauté pan on the stove with the Gorgonzola Sauce on low to keep warm.
8   Once the gnocchi have risen to the top, use a slotted spoon or skimmer to remove them to the sauté pan with the Gorgonzola Sauce. When all the gnocchi are cooked, turn the heat for the pan up to medium-high and stir gently with the sauce until the consistency is thick and coats the gnocchi.

To serve

Serve immediately. The gnocchi are also good served instead with Mamma's Pomodoro "Tomato Sauce" (see page 173).

NOTES: To freeze gnocchi for later use, just cook as directed above. As they rise to the surface use a slotted spoon or skimmer to remove them to a bowl of ice water. Once they have cooled (about two minutes) drain them briefly on paper towels.

Then lay them in a single layer on a parchment-lined baking sheet. Store them in the refrigerator if they will be used shortly (up to a day), or place them in the freezer.

Once they are frozen, remove them from the baking sheet and store them in well-sealed plastic bags. They can be kept frozen for several weeks. To cook them, add them to a hot sauce while they are still frozen. Do not thaw ahead of time.

Italy's traditional potato dumplings. –Damian

Damian always makes the best dumplings. They're so light. –Johnny

The trick is not overworking the dough. That's the only secret you need to keep them light and delicious. –Damian

Plus, you can make them ahead of time and freeze them. –Johnny

Left to right: "The Palazzo Cousins" Lucy Mandola, Bonnie Zarzana, Rosie Agnes Carrabba, Josephine Lacorte, Grandma Mary Carrabba, Lena Lanzo, Nita Petronella, Annie Alfano, Mary Cemino and Nita Carrabba

Desserts
Dolci

When it comes time for dessert around our families, things can get seriously out of hand. For one thing, even when everybody knows someone else is doing the cooking, we just can't stop folks from baking and bringing an extra dessert.

Among these recipes, and especially among the stories that go along with them, you'll find the desserts we loved growing up made by people who really loved to make dessert. Desserts were always no-holds-barred. It wasn't as though they had to be expensive—most, in fact, were not. But it was in these pies and cakes and tarts that the love really showed. And the love, even in hard times, didn't pinch pennies!

One of these photos shows Johnny's grandmother Mary Carrabba with a Model A Ford, right where they lived and ran a grocery store on a street called West Dallas. In the middle of Houston, naturally. She was a nice little cook. The other picture shows Grandma and Grandpa Mandola in front of their house. Their dinner table was known for its terrific desserts.

left to right:

Lucy Palazzo Mandola, Lena Lamonte Mandola, Grace Testa Mandola, Grandpa Vincenzo (Vincent) Mandola, Frances Mandola Corona, Margaret Mandola Lampasas, Grandma Margaret Romano Mandola, Sammy Mandola and Vincent Lampasas

Pears Poached in Red Wine

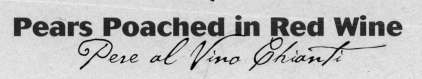

Pears Poached in Red Wine
Pere al Vino Chianti

SERVES 6

6	large, firm pears, preferably Bosc, with stems
4	cups good quality Chianti wine
1	cup Tawny port
1	cup cold water
1/2	lemon
1	cinnamon stick
6	tablespoons sugar

TO PREPARE

1 Peel the pears, then flatten the bottoms by cutting off a thin slice of each. Stand the pears up in a large metal saucepan. Don't overcrowd the pan.

2 Add the wine, port and water to the pears. Squeeze the half lemon and cut off a slice of peel. Add the juice and the peel to the pan, along with the cinnamon and sugar.

3 Cover the pan with foil or a lid and let simmer on low heat for 25 minutes. Test with a toothpick to be sure the pears are well cooked before removing from the flame.

4 Transfer the cooked pears to a serving platter, cover and let cool.

5 Remove the lemon peel from the liquid and reduce the sauce to the consistency of a light syrup, approximately 30 minutes on medium heat.

To serve

Place the pears on a platter, or individual serving plates and pour some of the sauce over each, sprinkle with lemon zest curls and serve. Fresh mascarpone, or other cheese, would go perfectly with these pears.

Italians love to eat fresh fruit for dessert, especially after a heavy meal. –Damian

And after you make these pears, you can purée any leftovers with the syrup and make them into a great Italian ice. –Johnny

Uncle Lee Ditta

Battered Fried Strawberries
Frittura di Fragoli

SERVES 4

BATTER INGREDIENTS

1 1/2	cups all-purpose flour
	A pinch of salt
2	teaspoons extra-virgin olive oil
1	extra large egg
2	extra large eggs, separated
1	cup cold water
1	tablespoon sugar
3	tablespoons Sambuca

STRAWBERRY INGREDIENTS

12	strawberries, de-stemmed, washed and dried
2	tablespoons sugar
1	dash lemon juice
1	tablespoon Sambuca
3	cups vegetable oil for deep frying
	Candied orange zest, chopped, for garnish

TO PREPARE THE BATTER

1 Place the flour and salt in a bowl and mix together well.

2 Make a well in the center of the flour mixture and add the olive oil, whole egg and egg yolks. Start stirring while adding the cold water, drizzling it in until fully incorporated and the mixture has no lumps.

3 Add the sugar and Sambuca. Let the batter rest for two hours in a cool place, but do not refrigerate.

4 To finish the batter, beat the egg whites until firm peaks form. Gently fold the egg whites into the batter.

TO PREPARE THE STRAWBERRIES

1 Mix the sugar, lemon juice and Sambuca together. Add this mixture to the strawberries and let marinate for one hour.

2 In a 1 1/2-quart (1.5 l) saucepan, preheat the vegetable oil to 350° F (180° C).

3 Dip the marinated strawberries in the finished batter and fry in the oil until golden brown, about one to two minutes. Drain on a paper-towel-lined plate.

To serve

Garnish with the chopped candied orange zest (found packaged in most food stores) and serve.

At first, you might never think of frying fresh fruit. But once you do it, you'll think of it from now on. –Damian

It's like fruit tempura, right? –Johnny

It's called a pastela batter. It couldn't get much simpler. I'm pretty sure it made its way to Sicily from North Africa, both as a recipe and as a name. –Damian

Oranges Marissa
Francie Marissa

SERVES 4–6

6	oranges
1	large lemon
3	cups water, plus enough water to boil the orange peel
1	cup + 3 tablespoons dry white wine
1 1/3	cups sugar
3	whole cloves
3	tablespoons Grand Marnier liqueur
	Fresh mint leaves for garnish

TO PREPARE

1 Strip the skin from the oranges and lemon from top to bottom, being careful to pull off just the peel and not the white pith. Cut the peel into very thin julienne. Set the oranges aside and save the lemon for another use.

2 Bring the water to a boil. Add the orange and lemon peel and boil for five minutes. Drain and transfer to a medium-sized, non-aluminum saucepan.

3 Add the 3 cups of water, 1 cup of wine, sugar and cloves to the saucepan. Bring to a boil, then lower the heat to medium and cook until a syrupy consistency and a medium caramel color, about 45 to 50 minutes.

4 Remove from heat and stir in the remaining 3 tablespoons of wine and the Grand Marnier.

5 Peel away all the white pith from the reserved oranges. At this point you can either cut segments from the oranges, cut slices across them or leave them whole, depending on your presentation preference.

To serve

Arrange the oranges in a serving bowl, top with the orange and lemon peel and pour the syrup over. Garnish with more peel, fresh mint and berry slices if you wish.

This dessert is named after Damian's daughter. –Johnny

I made oranges this way a lot back at D'Amico's, the restaurant I owned in the '70s. They're really, really good. –Damian

133

Fresh Peaches Stuffed with Amaretti Cookie Filling

Fresh Peaches Stuffed with Amaretti Cookie Filling

Pesche Ripiene

SERVES 6

6	firm but ripe peaches
6	Amaretti cookies, wrapped in a towel and crushed
2	tablespoons sugar
1	teaspoon cocoa powder, unsweetened
2	egg yolks
1	tablespoon Amaretto liqueur
3	tablespoons unsalted butter
1	teaspoon cinnamon
1/2	cup whipping cream, whipped

TO PREPARE

1 Preheat the oven to 375° F (190° C).

2 Cut the peaches in half and remove the pits. Scoop enough peach pulp out of each half to make a deep space in the center, leaving 1/4 inch (6 mm) of flesh.

3 To make the Amaretti mixture, chop the peach pulp fine and place in a mixing bowl. Add the crushed Amaretti cookies. Then stir in the sugar, cocoa, egg yolks and Amaretto liqueur.

4 Stuff the peach halves with the Amaretti mixture.

5 Arrange the peaches side by side in a buttered 8 x 10-inch (20 x 25 cm) baking dish.

6 Dot the peaches with the butter, sprinkle with the cinnamon and bake for about 12 to 15 minutes, or until they are just tender.

7 Baste with the syrup from the pan during the baking process.

To serve

Transfer two peach halves onto each individual serving plate. Serve hot or cold, topped with whipped cream.

Some people wonder why we're serving fish for dessert. But no, this is pesche, not pesce. Of course, the two words sound a lot alike. –Johnny

The important thing here is not words but peaches, and you have to use really ripe ones at the height of the season. Fredricksburg, Texas, grows great peaches, by the way. –Damian

Warm Custard Sauce with Raspberries
Zabaglione con Lamponi

DOLCI

SERVES 4–6

8	large egg yolks, room temperature
1/2	cup sugar
1/2	cup white wine
1/2	cup framboise or Chambord liqueur
3	pints fresh raspberries, or your favorite berries

The French call this sabayon. But they probably got the idea from us Italians.

—Damian

This is a little variation on traditional zabaglione, a perfect accent for whatever fresh berries you have around the house.

—Johnny

TO PREPARE

1 In the bottom half of a double boiler, bring a small amount of water to a simmer. In the top half of the double boiler, whisk the egg yolks and sugar until a creamy consistency and pale yellow in color.
2 Place the egg mixture over the simmering water and add the wine and framboise, whisking rapidly until they are well incorporated.
3 Continue beating well with a whisk until it begins to thicken and become fluffy, about four to six minutes. Remove from the heat and set aside.

To serve

Place the raspberries on a serving platter or in shallow bowls and spoon the mixture over the berries while still warm. You may use any berries you like.

You could serve the dessert as described above or sprinkle with granulated sugar and place under a broiler until golden brown, or use a torch and brown the top, making sure not to burn the custard. Serve immediately. Make sure that the bowls or platter you use can go into the oven; or, you may serve this dessert without browning the top.

136

Raspberry and Nectarine Crumble

Torta della Nettarina e Lampone

SERVES 6–8

CRUMB TOPPING INGREDIENTS

1/2	cup all-purpose flour
1/2	cup medium-grain, stone-ground cornmeal
1/3	cup light brown sugar, firmly packed
	Zest of one lime
	A pinch of salt
1/2	cup rolled oats
8	tablespoons unsalted butter, cubed and chilled

FRUIT INGREDIENTS

6	nectarines, sliced
2	pints (4 cups) fresh raspberries
	Juice of one lime
1/2	cup sugar
1/4	teaspoon freshly-grated nutmeg

TO PREPARE

1 Preheat oven to 375° F (190° C).
2 Butter an 11 x 8-inch (28 x 20 cm) baking dish and set aside.

TO PREPARE THE CRUMB TOPPING

In a large bowl, combine all the ingredients, using your fingers to work in the cold butter until the topping resembles a pebble-like texture, or using an electric mixer to achieve the same result. Refrigerate until ready to use.

TO PREPARE THE FRUIT AND FINISH

1 In another large bowl, add the fruit, lime juice, sugar and nutmeg. Toss gently, then transfer the mixture into the buttered baking dish.
2 Sprinkle the crumb topping over it evenly.
3 Bake for about 30 minutes until the topping is brown and bubbly. Cool for 10 minutes.

To serve

Spoon into individual serving bowls with a scoop of vanilla ice cream on top.

Any crumble is a good crumble. –Johnny

You can do all kinds of crumbles with plums, peaches, apples, pears, berries or combinations. But I happen to love nectarines. –Damian

Italian Cream Pudding with Dried Fig Compote

Panna Cotta con Fichi Sciroppata

SERVES 6

PANNA COTTA INGREDIENTS

1	cup whole milk
2³/4	teaspoons powdered gelatin
6	tablespoons sugar
2	teaspoons vanilla extract
1/8	teaspoon salt
3	cups heavy cream
1/8	cup mascarpone cheese
1/8	cup sour cream
2	teaspoons Frangelico liqueur

FIG COMPOTE INGREDIENTS

1	cup dried figs, cut in half and stems removed
3/4	cup sugar
1	cup white wine
1	cup Sauterne wine

TO PREPARE THE PANNA COTTA

1 Pour the milk into a medium saucepan. Sprinkle the gelatin powder over the top and let stand for 10 minutes to hydrate.

2 Meanwhile, make an ice water bath using two trays of ice cubes and 4 cups of cold water in a very large bowl. Set aside.

3 Heat the milk and gelatin mixture over high heat, stirring constantly until the gelatin is dissolved and the mixture registers 135° F (57° C), about 1¹/2 minutes.

4 Remove from the heat and stir in the sugar, vanilla and salt until dissolved, about one minute.

5 Stirring constantly, slowly add the heavy cream to the same pan. Add the mascarpone, sour cream and Frangelico, and stir until smooth. Transfer the mixture to a medium bowl and set over the ice bath.

6 Stir the mixture about 10 minutes until an eggnog consistency.

7 Pour the custard into ramekins or wine glasses. Cover with plastic wrap and chill about four hours or overnight.

TO PREPARE THE FIG COMPOTE

1 Place all the ingredients in a medium saucepan and bring to a low boil.

2 Simmer for 15 to 20 minutes, or until the consistency is thick and syrupy.

3 You can make the Fig Compote well in advance, store in an airtight container in the refrigerator, and reheat before serving. It should keep its freshness for up to 10 days in the refrigerator.

To serve

Unmold the pudding by dipping the ramekin into hot water for 20 to 30 seconds to loosen the edges. (You might need a small paring knife to help with this endeavor.) Turn out onto small serving dishes and drizzle the dried fig compote over the top and around the sides.

There aren't any eggs in this, so it's not a custard. –Damian

But it is a cooked cream. –Johnny

It's been around for years and years, and all of a sudden it's become very popular. It's especially good with this dried fig compote. –Damian

Nonna Testa's Milk Pudding
Bianca Mangiare alla Nonna Testa

SERVES 6–8

3	rounded tablespoons all-purpose flour
2	eggs
1/2	cup sugar
4	cups milk
	Freshly-grated nutmeg for garnish

TO PREPARE

1 Place the flour in the top portion of a 2-quart (2 l) double boiler. Beat in the eggs until well mixed. Add the sugar and beat well. Then gradually add the milk, stirring constantly so as not to form lumps.

2 Place the top portion of the double boiler over hot, but not boiling, water. Cook the custard, stirring constantly, until a thick, pudding-like consistency.

3 Pour into a serving platter and grate the nutmeg (to taste) over the custard. Make sure that your platter is not flat and has a high enough lip to hold in the pudding. Refrigerate until ready to serve.

To serve

Place in bowls or serve it family-style with your favorite berries, such as raspberries, blackberries or blueberries.

Here's a pudding my Grandma Testa made. My Grandma Mandola made a similar chocolate version. When I was a kid I'd take a nap at Grandma Mandola's and wake up to the smell of cinnamon and chocolate. –Damian

This one's all white, though. And all wonderful! –Johnny

Left to right: Aunt Frances Mandola Corona, Uncle Charlie Corona, unknown employee and Vincenzo Mandola in Grandpa and Grandma Mandola's grocery at the corner of Leland and Palmer Streets, in the 3rd Ward, Houston, Texas

Baked Custard with Caramel Sauce
Flan

SERVES 8

CARAMEL SAUCE INGREDIENTS
2   cups sugar
²/₃ cup water

CUSTARD INGREDIENTS
7   egg yolks
1   14-ounce (397 g) can sweetened condensed milk
1   12-ounce (340 g) can evaporated milk
2¹/₂ teaspoons vanilla extract
1¹/₃ cups heavy cream (buy 1 pint and you will have some left over)
¹/₄ teaspoon of cinnamon
      A pinch of salt

TO PREPARE THE CARAMEL SAUCE

1 Stir the sugar and water together in a medium saucepan.

2 Bring to a boil on medium-high heat while swirling the pan over the heat to dissolve the sugar—don't stir the mixture. Cover tightly and boil for seven to eight minutes, until the bubbles are thick and large.

3 Uncover and continue boiling, swirling the pan constantly in a circular motion. Once the color begins to darken, continue to cook for approximately one minute longer, until light brown in color.

4 Remove from the heat and keep swirling the pan, as the caramel will continue to darken.

5 Divide the caramel between 8 4-ounce (115 g) glass custard cups or porcelain ramekins. Turn the cups to coat the bottom and halfway up the sides with the caramel. Set aside.

Sicilians eat caramel custard, or crème caramel, all the time. –Damian

So do the Spanish, though, and somehow it's their name for it that won out. Flan is a classic. –Johnny

TO PREPARE THE CUSTARD

1 Preheat the oven to 300° F (150° C).

2 Combine all the ingredients in a large mixing bowl. Whisk well and strain through a wire mesh strainer or cheesecloth.

3 Pour the custard into the cups, leaving ¹/₈-inch (3 mm) room at the top.

4 Place the filled cups on a large baking sheet with at least one-inch (2.5 cm) sides. Fill up about ³/₄ inch with hot water.

5 Bake for 1–1¹/₂ hours until the edges are just set and the center is still slightly liquid. Remove from the oven and cool for 15 minutes. Cover and refrigerate for at least two hours or overnight.

To serve

Run a small paring knife around the edge of the cup. Place an individual serving plate over each cup and invert. The custard should come loose onto the plate with the caramel sauce coating the top and sides.

Almond and Kahlua Semi-Frozen Cream

Semifreddo con Amaretti e Kahlua

SERVES 6–8

14 egg yolks
$^2/_3$ cup sugar
$^1/_3$ cup Amaretto liqueur
$^1/_3$ cup almonds, coarsely chopped
$2^1/_2$ cups heavy cream, (1 pint) whipped until stiff
$^1/_3$ cup cocoa, unsweetened
$^1/_3$ cup Kahlua

TO PREPARE

1 In a large saucepan or the bottom half of a double boiler, put about one inch (2.5 cm) of water and place on high heat to boil.

2 Butter a standard $4^1/_2$ x 8-inch (11.5 x 20 cm) loaf pan and line with plastic wrap, leaving a two-inch (5 cm) overhang on the narrow ends.

FOR THE FIRST LAYER

1 In the top half of the double boiler or medium mixing bowl, add 7 egg yolks and $^1/_3$ cup sugar and beat for approximately five minutes until the mixture forms a ribbon.

2 Place the bowl on top of the boiling water but make sure not to let it touch the water. Add the Amaretto and whisk until thick, about another five to seven minutes.

3 Remove from the heat and set the bowl on ice. Stir occasionally until cooled. Fold in the chopped almonds and half of the whipped cream, about $1^1/_4$ cups.

4 Pour the mixture into the prepared loaf pan and place in the freezer to set up for about 30 to 45 minutes until firm but not frozen through.

FOR THE SECOND LAYER

1 Check the level of the water in the bottom half of the double boiler and add more if needed. Bring water back to a boil.

A semifreddo, meaning "somewhat cold," is not a full-fledged ice cream. It's lighter than that. –Damian

You can make semifreddo with fruit or chocolate or nuts, and each time it'll have a totally different texture. –Johnny

2 In the top half of the double boiler or medium mixing bowl, add the remaining egg yolks and $^1/_3$ cup sugar and beat for approximately five minutes until the mixture forms a ribbon.

3 Place the bowl on top of the boiling water but make sure not to let it touch the water. Add the Kahlua and whisk until thick, about another five to seven minutes.

4 Remove from the heat and set the bowl on ice. Stir occasionally until cooled. Fold in the cocoa and the remaining whipped cream.

5 Pour the mixture into the loaf pan on top of the first layer. Cover with plastic wrap and freeze for four to six hours.

To serve

Remove from the freezer and peel the plastic wrap away from the top of the custard. Turn the frozen custard out onto a platter and remove the plastic wrap. Cut into 1–$1^1/_2$-inch (2.5–4 cm) thick slices and serve immediately.

Almond Ice Cream
Gelato di Mandorla

SERVE 6–8

This recipe requires an ice cream maker.

4   ounces (115 g) almond paste
2/3   cup sugar + 1 tablespoon sugar
3   eggs
1/2   teaspoon almond extract
1/4   teaspoon salt
2   cups half-and-half
1   cup heavy cream
1/2   cup Amaretto liqueur
1   cup amaretti cookies, crumbled

TO PREPARE

1   In a large mixing bowl with an electric mixer, combine the almond paste and sugar and beat until smooth.

2   Add the eggs one at a time, beating well after each addition. Beat in the almond extract and salt.

3   In a medium saucepan, bring the half-and-half to a simmer over medium heat. Slowly beat the hot half-and-half into the almond paste mixture.

4   Pour the entire mixture back into the saucepan and place over low heat. Stir constantly with a whisk until the custard thickens. Do not let it boil or the eggs will scramble.

5   Remove from the heat and pour the hot custard through a wire mesh strainer or cheesecloth into a large, clean bowl. Allow the custard to cool until room temperature.

6   Stir in the heavy cream and the Amaretto liqueur. Cover and refrigerate at least three to four hours or overnight.

7   When you're ready to make the ice cream, stir the crumbled amaretti cookies into the chilled custard and follow the manufacturer's instructions for your ice cream maker.

8   You may need to do this in two batches depending on the capacity of your ice cream maker.

To serve

Scoop out the desired portion into your favorite bowl. Most Italians eat gelato plain, but you can always add a piece of cake or pie.

After a big lunch in Italy, we never have dessert in a restaurant. –Johnny

One of our favorite things to do is hit the street for gelato. It's so much creamier and softer than American ice cream. –Damian

And it's everywhere in Italy. –Johnny

Everybody's walking around with a cone in their hand. –Damian

Chocolate Ricotta Cheesecake
Crostata di Ricotta

MAKES ONE 10-INCH (25 CM) CHEESECAKE

1	Rich Pie Crust (see page 169)
1/2	cup golden raisins, chopped
8	ounces (225 g) semisweet chocolate
4	tablespoons spiced rum
1	pound fresh Ricotta Cheese (see page 176)
1/2	cup sugar
1	tablespoon flour

4	eggs, separated
1/4	cup whipping cream
1/4	cup sour cream
1	teaspoon vanilla extract
1	teaspoon grated orange zest
1/4	teaspoon salt

TO PREPARE

1 Prepare the crust and chill for one hour.

2 Right before you mix the filling, roll out the chilled dough and line a buttered, 2-inch (5 cm) deep spring-form cake pan.

3 Press the crust evenly into the bottom of the cake pan and 3/4 of the way up the sides. Return to refrigerator until you are ready to fill the shell.

4 Preheat the oven to 350° F (180° C).

5 Soak the raisins in the rum for 1/2 hour. Drain the liquor and reserve.

6 Melt the chocolate over a double boiler gently. Set aside to cool slightly.

7 Beat the ricotta cheese until smooth. Add the sugar and flour and continue to mix until creamy. Then add the egg yolks, whipping cream, sour cream, vanilla, orange zest and reserved rum. Mix until well incorporated.

8 Add the melted chocolate and the drained raisins. Set aside.

9 In a mixer, beat the egg whites and salt to stiff peaks.

10 Fold 1/3 of the egg whites at a time, into the cheese mixture, being careful not to overmix the filling.

11 Pour the filling into the crust shell and smooth out the top.

12 Bake for 50 to 60 minutes. Turn off the oven and let the cake cool inside the oven with the door ajar for another 30 minutes. Continue to let the cake cool well before cutting. Refrigerate after cooling.

To serve

Dip a slender knife first into hot water before cutting. Place the slices on individual serving plates.

I love cheesecake. This one is an Italian version. –Damian

It's a little bit grainier with the ricotta, but it's got a wonderful flavor. –Johnny

And it's especially good a little warm. –Damian

Fried Pastry Tubes with Ricotta Filling
Cannoli

MAKES ABOUT 12–18 CANNOLI

PASTRY TUBE INGREDIENTS

2	cups all-purpose flour
1	tablespoon sugar
1	teaspoon cinnamon
1	tablespoon Crisco shortening (regular flavor) or lard
1	egg
1/2	teaspoon vanilla extract
1/2	cup sweet red wine or sweet Marsala
1	quart (1l) vegetable oil for frying

FILLING INGREDIENTS

1 1/2	pounds (750 g) whole milk ricotta cheese, drained in a strainer lined with cheesecloth for at least two hours
1 1/2	cups powdered sugar
1/4	cup diced candied fruit
1/2	teaspoon vanilla extract
1/4	cup mini chocolate chips
1/4	cup chopped pistachios
	Powdered sugar for garnish
	Candied cherries for garnish, cut in half

TO PREPARE THE PASTRY TUBES

1 Sift the flour, sugar and cinnamon into a bowl.

2 Cut in the Crisco and rub into the flour mixture. Add the egg and vanilla. Add enough wine to make a firm dough. (Do not add all of the wine at one time—it may not all be necessary.)

3 Knead the dough until firm and elastic. Cover with plastic wrap and let rest for 30 minutes.

4 In a 3-quart (2.75 l) pan or Dutch oven, preheat the oil to 350° F (180° C).

5 Roll the dough paper-thin on a counter top and cut into equal squares. Place a metal tube (available in most kitchen stores) diagonally on each square and bring the two corners over to meet in the middle. Press gently to seal.

6 To fry the shells, gently drop them a few at a time into the hot oil and cook until they are a deep golden brown. Remove them with tongs.

7 Immediately slide the shells off the metal tubes by gripping one end of the cylinder with tongs and using a mitt-covered hand or paper towel, gently gripping the shell and twisting and pulling at the same time. Cool the shells on absorbent paper.

TO PREPARE THE FILLING

1 In a mixing bowl, beat the ricotta and sugar until smooth.

2 Add the remaining ingredients and blend well.

3 Immediately before serving, using a pastry bag with no tube on the end, fill the cannoli with the ricotta mixture.

To serve

Sprinkle with powdered sugar and place a candied cherry half, or other candied fruit, on each end.

We had an Aunt Phil Dorsa in Dallas who made great cannoli. When we drove up to Dallas, she'd always have cannoli waiting for us. It was the first thing we ate. –Johnny

Cannoli is the quintessential Sicilian pastry. I remember being in Sicily with my brothers and sisters, in Corleone where some of my family is from. We were having lunch and I asked for cannoli for dessert. I remember the proprietor sent a boy out for some cannoli from this little pastry shop and told him, "If the ricotta wasn't made this morning, don't get any." That turned out to be the best cannoli I ever had. –Damian

Lemon Rosemary Pound Cake
Torta di Rosmarino e Limone

SERVES 6–8

SYRUP INGREDIENTS
1/3–1/2 cup sugar
2   sprigs rosemary
     Juice of 3 whole lemons

CAKE INGREDIENTS
1 1/2 cups flour
1/4   teaspoon baking soda
1/4   teaspoon baking powder

1/4   teaspoon salt
      Grated zest of 2 whole lemons
2   teaspoons chopped fresh rosemary
8   tablespoons softened butter
1   cup sugar
1/2   teaspoon vanilla
2   eggs
1/2   cup buttermilk

TO PREPARE THE SYRUP

1 In a small saucepan, bring the sugar, rosemary and lemon juice to a boil over medium-high heat.
2 Cook for five to ten minutes until the sugar is melted and you have a syrup-like consistency. Keep warm and set aside.

TO PREPARE THE CAKE

1 Preheat the oven to 350° F (180° C).
2 Grease and flour a standard 4 1/2 x 8-inch (11.5 x 20 cm) loaf pan.
3 In a bowl, stir together the flour, baking soda, baking powder, salt, lemon zest and rosemary. Set aside.
4 In another bowl, cream together the butter and sugar until fluffy.
5 Mix in the vanilla and the eggs one at a time until fully incorporated.
6 Stir in the flour mixture and buttermilk, alternating with one third of each at a time. Mix well and pour into the prepared loaf pan.

7 Put in the oven and bake for about 30 minutes, or until a toothpick inserted in the middle comes out clean. Remove from the oven and cool for 10 minutes.
8 Turn out onto a serving cake or platter and make about a dozen holes on top with a toothpick. Pour the warm syrup over the top.

To serve

Cut into 1/2-inch (1.5 cm) slices and serve warm or at room temperature.

Rosemary sounds kind of funny in a pound cake. –Johnny

But it really is delicious! –Damian

Serve it warm. –Johnny

Apple Cake
Torta di Mele

SERVES 9

CAKE INGREDIENTS

$^1/_2$	cup whole milk ricotta cheese
8	tablespoons butter, softened
1	cup sugar
1	egg, beaten
1	cup flour
1	teaspoon baking powder
$^1/_2$	teaspoon salt
$^1/_2$	teaspoon cinnamon
3	apples, peeled, cored and grated (you should have 2$^1/_2$ cups grated apples)
$^1/_2$	cup pecans, toasted and coarsely chopped

CHANTILLY CREAM INGREDIENTS

2	cups heavy whipping cream
$^1/_2$	cup powdered sugar
$^1/_4$	cup bourbon or any other liqueur

I guess by now everybody knows Johnny and I love simple cakes. –Damian

Without a whole lot of icing. –Johnny

This one reminds me of home and Grandma, which are real good things for a cake to remind you of. –Damian

⌒ In the Testa Cola plant.

TO PREPARE THE CAKE

1 Preheat the oven to 350° F (180° C).

2 Grease and flour a 9 x 9-inch (23 x 23 cm) square pan.

3 In a bowl, cream together ricotta, butter and sugar until fluffy. Add 1 beaten egg and mix well.

4 Sift the flour, baking powder, salt and cinnamon into the ricotta mixture and mix well to combine. Fold in the apples and pecans.

5 Pour the cake batter into the prepared cake pan and bake for 35 minutes, or until golden brown and done in the center.

TO PREPARE THE CHANTILLY CREAM

1 In a chilled glass or stainless steel medium bowl, whip the heavy whipping cream until soft peaks form.

2 Add the powdered sugar and bourbon and whip until stiff.

To serve

Cut the cake into nine equal squares and place on individual serving plates. Serve warm or room temperature with a big spoonful of the chantilly cream.

Coconut Cake
Torta della Noce di Cocco

SERVES 8–10

CAKE INGREDIENTS

3 cups cake flour
4 teaspoons baking powder
1 teaspoon salt
1/2 pound (225 g) unsalted butter, softened
1 1/2 cups sugar
4 eggs, separated
1 cup milk
1 teaspoon vanilla extract
3/4 cup pecans, toasted and chopped

ICING INGREDIENTS

1/2 cup unsalted butter, room temperature
1 8-ounce (225 g) package cream cheese
3 cups powdered sugar, sifted
1 teaspoon vanilla extract
1 teaspoon coconut extract
2–4 tablespoons half-and-half
2 cups grated coconut

TO PREPARE THE CAKE

1 Preheat the oven to 350° F (180° C).
2 Grease and flour 2 9-inch (23 cm) round cake pans.
3 Sift the flour, baking powder and salt into a mixing bowl and set aside. In a large mixing bowl, cream together the butter and sugar until fluffy. Add the egg yolks one at a time, beating well after each addition.
4 Add the flour mixture and milk in thirds alternately with the sugar mixture, beating until smooth before adding the next. Mix in the vanilla and pecans. Beat the egg whites until stiff and fold into the batter.
5 Divide the batter evenly into the prepared pans.
6 Bake for 25 minutes until the center springs back slightly to the touch.
7 Let the cakes cool for 10 minutes, then turn them out onto cooling racks.

TO PREPARE THE ICING

1 In a mixing bowl, cream together the butter and cream cheese.
2 Gradually beat in the powdered sugar. Beat in the vanilla and coconut extracts.
3 Beat in as much of the half-and-half as desired to achieve a smooth, spreadable frosting.
4 Ice one cake on top and sides. Sprinkle liberally with coconut. Top with second cake and continue icing and adding coconut.

To serve

Cut into wedges and serve on individual plates.

I wanted to do a coconut cake for the book because I love coconut cake. Mamma always made me one on my birthday. –Damian

I guess we really like old-fashioned desserts. –Johnny

What's not to like? –Damian

Rocky Road Cake

Rocky Road Cake
Torta della Strata Pitrusu

SERVES 10–12

CAKE INGREDIENTS

1 ¹/₂ cups flour
4 tablespoons cocoa powder
1 teaspoon baking powder
2 sticks butter, softened
2 cups sugar
2 teaspoons vanilla extract
1 tablespoon butter flavoring extract
4 eggs
2 cups pecans, coarsely chopped

ICING INGREDIENTS

1 4-ounce (115 g) stick butter, melted
4 tablespoons cocoa powder
¹/₂ cup canned evaporated milk
1 1-pound (450 g) box powdered sugar
1 10-ounce (275 g) bag mini marshmallows

TO PREPARE THE CAKE

1 Preheat the oven to 350° F (180° C).

2 Butter and flour a 9 x 13-inch (23 x 33 cm) cake pan.

3 Combine the flour, cocoa powder and baking powder. Set aside.

4 Cream together the butter, sugar, vanilla extract and butter flavoring extract. Beat in one egg at a time until fully incorporated.

5 Add the flour mixture, a little at a time, and fold the pecans in at the end. Pour the batter into the prepared cake pan. Bake for 25 to 35 minutes.

TO PREPARE THE ICING

1 In a medium saucepan, combine the melted butter, cocoa powder, canned evaporated milk and powdered sugar. Cook on the stove top for approximately 10 to 15 minutes. The icing is ready when you can drop a small amount of it in a cup of cold water, swirl it with your finger and a ball will form.

2 When it's reached the softball stage, stir in the marshmallows until smooth. Pour on top of the cake, spreading evenly to cover.

To serve

Let the iced cake sit for 30 minutes and then cut into the desired pieces.

Our cousin Jo Francis Corona always made marshmallow and nut desserts. –Damian

This recipe is a tribute to her. –Johnny

It's kind of like Rocky Road ice cream, except better. –Damian

If you want, you can use large marshmallows—like we did on the show—in place of the minis. This way there will be some chunks of marshmallow in the icing. –Johnny

"Pick Me Up" Cake
Tiramisù

SERVES 9

2	eggs, separated
6	tablespoons granulated sugar
1	pound (40 g) mascarpone cheese
1	tablespoon Meyers Rum
1/2	teaspoon vanilla extract
2	cups espresso coffee
2	tablespoons Frangelico liqueur
2	tablespoons Tia Maria liqueur
2	7-ounce (200 g) packages plain ladyfingers, soft or dried
7	ounces (200 g) semisweet chocolate, grated

TO PREPARE

1 Place the egg yolks and sugar in a 5-quart (4.75 l) mixer. Beat them together on medium speed until well blended, pale in color and slightly thickened.

2 Add the mascarpone and beat until smooth. Reduce the speed, add the rum and vanilla and blend until well mixed.

3 In a separate bowl, beat the egg whites until stiff. Fold half of the egg whites into the mascarpone mixture.

4 In a separate mixing bowl, combine the espresso, Frangelico and Tia Maria.

5 Dip the ladyfingers into the espresso mixture and use them to line the bottom and sides of a 9 x 9-inch (23 x 23 cm) casserole dish.

6 Place half of the Mascarpone mixture over the ladyfingers.

7 Sprinkle half of the chocolate evenly over the first layer of the tiramisù.

8 Repeat with the dipped ladyfingers, the remainder of the Mascarpone mixture, and the remainder of the chocolate to finish.

9 Cover tightly with plastic wrap and refrigerate overnight.

To serve

Use a large spoon to scoop out into individual serving bowls. Or you can serve it family-style by scooping it out at the table.

Does everybody know what *tiramisù* means by now? –Damian

I don't know, Big D. You might try them. –Johnny

It means "pick me up," a reference to the espresso in this dessert. It comes with its own cup of coffee. –Damian

The key here is not over-whipping the mascarpone. –Johnny

We want it to be real light and soft— –Damian

So it melts in your mouth. –Johnny

Trio Layer Cake
Torta Tre Sapori

MAKES ONE 9-INCH (23 CM) CAKE

VANILLA BATTER INGREDIENTS

3	cups cake flour
3 1/4	teaspoons baking powder
3/4	teaspoon salt
1 1/2	sticks (6 ounces) (175 g) unsalted butter
1 3/4	cups sugar
4	eggs
1	cup milk
1	teaspoon vanilla

SPICE INGREDIENTS

3/4	teaspoon cinnamon
1/2	teaspoon allspice
1/4	teaspoon cloves
1/4	nutmeg, grated

CHOCOLATE BATTER INGREDIENTS

2	teaspoons sugar
2	teaspoons unsalted butter, melted
1	ounce (30 g) unsweetened chocolate, melted and cooled
1/8	teaspoon baking soda
1 1/2	tablespoons hot water
1	recipe Vanilla Cream Filling (see page 177)
1	recipe Chocolate Frosting (see page 177)

TO PREPARE THE BATTERS

1 Preheat the oven to 375° F (190° C).

2 Grease 3 9-inch (23 cm) round cake pans and line the bottoms with parchment paper.

3 In a bowl, sift together the flour, baking powder and salt. Sift again two more times. Set aside.

4 In a separate bowl, cream the butter until light and fluffy and then gradually beat in the sugar until well mixed.

5 Add the eggs one at a time, beating well after each addition.

6 Gradually, add the flour mixture to the butter mixture, alternating it with the milk and the vanilla. Mix well after each addition.

7 Now divide the batter into three parts, putting it into separate mixing bowls.

8 Add all the spices to one of the bowls of batter and mix well. Set aside.

9 To the second bowl of batter, add all the chocolate ingredients and mix well. Leave the third bowl of vanilla batter as is.

TO FINISH

1 Turn each of the batters separately into the prepared cake pans.

2 Bake all three at once for 30 minutes. Remove them from the oven and let cool 10 minutes. Then remove the layers from the pans and cool another 20 minutes until they are room temperature.

3 Spread the Vanilla Cream Filling between the layers and stack the layers in any order you desire, then cover the top and the sides with the Chocolate Frosting.

To serve

Cut into wedges and place on individual serving plates.

My mother made this cake all the time, with a chocolate layer, a spice layer and a vanilla layer. –Damian

It's real simple. I always eat about four slices. –Johnny

Jelly Roll
Torta Marmellata Arrotolata

SERVES 8–10

CAKE INGREDIENTS

4 egg yolks
3/4 cup sugar
1 teaspoon almond extract
1/4 cup hot espresso or very strong coffee
4 egg whites
A pinch of salt
1 cup cake flour
Powdered sugar, for dusting

FILLING INGREDIENTS

2/3 cup heavy whipping cream
1/2 teaspoon vanilla extract
2 teaspoons pure maple syrup
1 cup blackberry jam

TO PREPARE THE CAKE

1 Preheat the oven to 350° F (180° C).

2 Butter and line a 10^{1}/2 x 15^{1}/2-inch (26 x 39 cm) jelly roll pan with parchment paper.

3 Using a standing mixer with a whisk attachment, beat the egg yolks, 1/2 cup of the sugar, almond extract and the hot espresso on high until thick and tripled in volume, about six minutes.

4 In another bowl with a hand mixer, beat the egg whites with a pinch of salt. Sprinkle in the remaining 1/4 cup of sugar gradually. Mix on medium-high another two minutes until peaks are glossy and hold their shape.

5 Fold the whites into the yolk mixture in thirds. Gently sift the flour over the top and fold until incorporated. Pour the batter into the prepared jelly roll pan and gently smooth out the surface with a flat spatula.

6 Bake for 10 to 12 minutes. The cake is done when it springs back in the center with the touch of a finger. Remove from the oven and cool for five minutes.

7 Cut out a piece of parchment or wax paper to the same size as the jelly roll pan and dust with a little bit of powdered sugar.

8 Turn the cake out onto the dusted parchment and carefully peel off the baking parchment paper from the cake. Cool for five to ten more minutes.

TO PREPARE THE FILLING AND ASSEMBLE

1 Use a hand mixer or whisk to whip the whipping cream with the vanilla extract and maple syrup until light and fluffy.

2 Spread the jam evenly over the sponge cake, leaving a one-inch (2.5 cm) margin around the entire cake. Then spread the whipped cream over the jam.

3 Roll up the cake by taking hold of one of the short ends of the parchment paper beneath it. As you lift the paper, the cake will begin to come up. Gently roll it over, pulling the paper away as it rolls.

4 If the cake cracks a bit as you roll it, don't worry about it because it's all going to get covered with more powdered sugar.

5 Place the cake on a serving platter and put into the freezer for 15 minutes to firm up.

To serve

Dust with more powdered sugar—it's up to you how much you would like to use. We like a lot. Slice and serve on plates. This dessert goes great with a good cup of coffee.

My mother made this. —Damian

It's a fun cake because you have to roll it up. —Johnny

People don't make these kinds of cakes much anymore. But they're so good. —Damian

Domed Cake
Zuccotto

SERVES 8–10

CAKE INGREDIENTS

1   cup cake flour

4   eggs, separated

3/4   cup sugar, divided into 1/2 cup and 1/4 cup

1   teaspoon almond extract

1/4   cup espresso

    A pinch of salt

1/2   cup brandy

FILLING INGREDIENTS

3   cups heavy cream

1   cup powdered sugar

7   ounces (200 g) walnuts, coarsely chopped

6   ounces (175 g) cocoa powder

    Cocoa powder for garnish

    Powdered sugar for garnish

Zuccotto means "large pumpkin." But basically this is a domed cake, you know— –Damian

Like the Astrodome in Houston. –Johnny

Except sweeter. I used to make this all the time at D'Amico's and later at Damian's. –Damian

It's a little too high-tech for me. I will eat it, though. –Johnny

It's like a big bowl of whipped cream surrounded by cake. –Damian

TO PREPARE THE CAKE

1   Preheat the oven to 350° F (180° C). Set a rack in the middle level of the oven.

2   Butter a 10 1/2 x 15 1/2-inch (26 x 39 cm) jelly roll pan and line with parchment paper.

3   Place a sifter on a plate and pour the cake flour inside the sifter. Leave it still and set aside.

4   In the bowl of an electric mixer fitted with the whisk attachment, whip together the egg yolks and 1/2 cup of the sugar.

5   Add the almond extract on medium speed and mix for two to three minutes until light and fluffy. Stir in the espresso and set aside.

Houston City Champions 1946, the Fogle West Funeral Home Baseball Team, Tony Mandola (third from left holding bat, of players sitting on bumper) and Frank Mandola (3rd from the left of players on the running board).

[Continued]

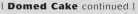

DOLCI

6   In a clean, dry mixer bowl fitted with a clean dry whisk attachment free from any oil or grease, whip the egg whites and salt on medium speed until white and opaque.

7   Whip in the remaining $1/4$ cup of sugar, one tablespoon at a time, and continue whipping until the egg whites hold a firm peak.

8   Using a large rubber spatula, fold the yolk mixture into the egg whites.

9   Sift the cake flour over the bowl $1/4$ of it at a time, and fold in after each addition. Scrape the batter into the prepared jelly roll pan and smooth the top.

10   Bake in the preheated oven until it is well risen, well colored and beginning to shrink away from the sides of the pan, about 10 to 12 minutes. Let cool.

11   Turn the cake out onto a cutting board, peel away the parchment paper and cut width-wise (across) into two- to three-inch (5 to 8 cm) strips.

12   Line a 2-quart (2 l) bowl with plastic wrap and then line the bowl with cake strips, fitting them snugly together or overlapping them slightly. There should be a few strips left over.

13   Sprinkle the cake-lined bowl with half the brandy to flavor the cake. Set aside.

TO PREPARE THE FILLING

1   In a large mixing bowl, whip the heavy cream with the powdered sugar.

2   Separate the whipped cream into two equal parts in separate mixing bowls.

3   Mix half of the whipped cream with the walnuts and place into the cake-lined bowl.

4   Mix the other half of the whipped cream with the cocoa powder and pour on top of the walnut–whipped cream mixture.

5   Put the rest of the cake strips on top to cover. Trim any overlapping pieces and drizzle with the remaining brandy. Cover with plastic and refrigerate for several hours or overnight.

To serve

Invert a platter on the bowl and turn out the cake onto the platter. Remove the bowl and the plastic wrap. Sift the cocoa powder and confectioner's sugar over the top to garnish. Cut into individual slices and serve.

Sicilian Doughnuts
Sfinci

MAKES ABOUT ONE DOZEN 1-INCH (2.5 CM) BALLS

	Vegetable oil for deep frying, approximately 1–2 quarts (1–2 l)
1	cup flour
1	tablespoon baking powder
3	tablespoons sugar
1/2	teaspoon cinnamon
1	egg
3/4	cup milk
	Powdered sugar for dusting or cinnamon-sugar (1 cup sugar blended with 2 tablespoons cinnamon)
	Warm honey

This is a little like a French beignet. –Johnny

Except it's Sicilian, and it's ours, so it's better. You need to watch how much milk you put in your sfinci batter. Making the batter thick gives you a nice ball to drop into the hot oil. –Damian

Hot desserts go over real well, especially with hot honey drizzled on top. –Johnny

TO PREPARE
1 Preheat about three to four inches (8–10 cm) of oil in a large saucepan to 350° F (180° C).
2 Mix the dry ingredients together thoroughly. Add the eggs and milk and beat until smooth.
3 Drop the thick batter by large tablespoons into the hot oil and fry until golden brown. Drain on paper towels.

To serve
Place on a plate and dust with powdered sugar or while still hot, roll in cinnamon-sugar. Drizzle honey over the top—then drizzle a little more if you want to look like us! Enjoy them while they're still hot.

Lena Vallone's Pecan Pie
Crostata di Noce alla Lena Vallone

MAKES ONE 9-INCH (23 CM) PIE

1   recipe Mamma's Pie Crust (see page 169)
2   ounces (50 g) butter, room temperature
1/2 cup sugar
3   eggs
1   cup white Karo syrup
1   teaspoon vanilla
     A pinch of salt
2   tablespoons all-purpose flour
2   cups pecans, chopped

DOLCI

You know what I like about this pie? This one's not real sticky sweet, like some pecan pies around the Deep South. Those pies just get "old" to me after a few bites. –Damian

I never eat a whole piece of pecan pie—I like to put it in the refrigerator and come back again and again for one bite at a time. –Johnny

Mrs. Vallone was a great baker. She moved to Atlanta and we sure have missed her around here. –Damian

TO PREPARE

1 Prepare the pie crust and chill for at least 30 minutes.

2 Preheat the oven to 350° F (180° C).

3 In a medium mixing bowl, cream the butter and sugar together. Add the eggs one at a time and beat thoroughly.

4 Add the syrup, vanilla and salt and sift in 2 tablespoons flour. Mix well.

5 Place Mamma's Pie Crust in a 9-inch (23 cm) glass pie dish (see page 171).

6 Place the pecans in the bottom of the pie shell. Then pour the batter over the pecans.

7 Bake the pie for 15 minutes, then lower the oven to 325° F (170° C) and bake another 40 to 45 minutes.

8 Check pie after 30 minutes to see if the pecans are browning too much. If so, cover the pie loosely with foil.

To serve

Cut into wedges and serve on individual serving plates. Plain whipped cream goes well with this pie.

Left to right: Damian's sisters Margaret Mandola Vallone, Rosie Mandola Carrabba and Mamma Grace Mandola.

Sweet Potato Tart
Crostata di Patata Dolci

MAKES ONE 10-INCH (25 CM) TART

1	recipe Rich Pie Crust (see page 169)
1	pound (450 g) red yams
1	pound (450 g) sweet potatoes
1/2	stick butter
2	eggs
1	egg yolk
2	teaspoons vanilla
1	cup heavy cream
1/2	cup light brown sugar
1/3	cup maple syrup
1 1/2	teaspoons salt
1 1/2	teaspoons cinnamon
1/2	teaspoon ground ginger
1/4	teaspoon freshly-grated nutmeg
	A pinch of white pepper

TO PREPARE

1 Prepare the crust and chill for one hour.

2 Preheat the oven to 400° F (200° C).

3 Roast the yams and potatoes until soft, about 50 to 60 minutes.

4 When cool enough to handle, peel off the skins and transfer them to a mixing bowl.

5 On low speed, add the butter and mix until it is melted and incorporated.

6 Turn the mixer up to medium and add the eggs and yolk one at a time, beating well after each addition.

7 Add the vanilla, cream, sugar, maple syrup, salt and spices. Mix until smooth.

8 Place the pie crust in a 10-inch (25 cm) tart pan (see page 169)

9 Fill the tart shell and smooth out the top.

10 Bake the tart on a sheet pan for 15 minutes. Then turn the temperature down to 350° F (180° C) and bake another 25 minutes.

To serve

Cut into wedges and serve on individual serving plates either warm or chilled. This is traditionally served around the holidays, but can be made whenever you can find some good sweet potatoes.

Using fresh sweet potatoes, which are sometimes called Louisiana yams, is real important to this dessert. –Damian

Boy, is this one good! –Johnny

Plum Tart

Plum Tart
Crostata di Prugne

SERVES 8–10

1 Rich Pie Crust (see page 169)
1/2 cup walnuts or other nuts
1/4 cup + 1 tablespoon sugar*
1/4 cup all-purpose flour
1–1 1/2 pounds (450–750 g) plums, halved, pitted and cut into 1/4-inch (6 mm) slices
  * If plums are sweet, cut down sugar by half
1/3 stick unsalted butter, cut into small pieces
1 tablespoon melted butter for crust
1 tablespoon plum brandy or other fruit liqueur
2 tablespoons red currant or seedless red raspberry jam

TO PREPARE

1 Prepare the crust and chill for one hour.

2 Preheat the oven to 400° F (200° C) and adjust the oven rack to the middle shelf.

3 In a food processor fitted with the metal blade, place the walnuts and 1/4 cup sugar. Turn the machine on and off twice and then process about 10 seconds.

4 Add the flour and process for about 10 more seconds to make a fine powder.

5 Line a 10 x 15-inch (25 cm x 38 cm) baking sheet with parchment paper.

6 On a lightly-floured surface, roll out the chilled dough into a rough rectangle about 1/8-inch (3 mm) thick. Loosely wrap onto your rolling pin and unwrap onto the parchment-lined baking sheet.

7 Spread the nut mixture evenly on the dough, leaving a one-inch (2.5 cm) border.

8 Neatly arrange the plums, overlapping slightly, on the dough. Fold the rim of the dough up over the outermost fruit and pinch together any tears or gaps.

9 Distribute the butter pieces evenly over the fruit. Sprinkle half of the remaining sugar evenly over the fruit and rim.

10 Brush the outside of the crust with melted butter and sprinkle the remaining sugar on the crust.

11 Bake for about 40 minutes or until the crust is golden. Remove from the oven and cool to lukewarm.

12 In a small saucepan over low heat, stir the brandy and the jam together. Heat just until it's melted and spoon evenly over the tart.

To serve
Cut into wedges and serve at room temperature.

I remember the first day Damian made this. He had perfect plums. That's the key to this recipe, along with serving it hot with vanilla bean ice cream. –Johnny

Italian prune plums are the best. –Damian

Date and Oatmeal Cookies
Russian Rocks

MAKES ABOUT TWO DOZEN COOKIES

$1/2$	cup shortening
$1/2$	cup sugar
$1/2$	cup dates, chopped
$1/2$	cup dark raisins, chopped
1	cup oatmeal
1	cup flour
$1/2$	teaspoon cinnamon
$1/4$	teaspoon nutmeg
$1/4$	teaspoon ground cloves
$1/4$	teaspoon allspice
$1/2$	teaspoon baking soda
$1/2$	cup pecans, coarsely chopped
2	tablespoons milk

Damian and I always say this is one of our favorite Christmas cookies. –Johnny

I don't know how it got the name of Russian Rocks. But the key is making the recipe so you have to squeeze the dough hard to get it to stick together. –Damian

TO PREPARE

1 Preheat the oven to 350° F (180° C).

2 Lightly grease a cookie sheet.

3 In a medium bowl, cream the shortening and sugar together with an electric mixer.

4 Add the dates and raisins and continue mixing for another minute.

5 Place the oatmeal in a large bowl and add the next six ingredients, sifted together. Mix until combined well.

6 Add the sugar and shortening mixture to the dry ingredients. Then add the pecans and milk and mix all the ingredients thoroughly by hand.

7 The texture of the dough should be like a coarse meal that, when moist enough, stays together when formed into a ball. If the dough is too dry, add another tablespoon of milk. Be careful not to make the dough too moist or the cookies will be too soft and not live up to the name "Russian Rocks."

8 Press the cookies together into $1/2$-inch (1.5 cm) balls and place on the prepared cookie sheet.

9 Bake for 20 to 25 minutes or until golden brown. The cookies will be soft while they are hot, but when they are completely cool, they will be very hard and crunchy. Store in an airtight container.

To serve

It is a tradition to have these cookies at Christmas time. Serve them by themselves or add them to your holiday cookie repertoire.

Sesame Seed Shortbread Cookies
Giuggiulena

MAKES ABOUT THREE DOZEN COOKIES

2 1/2 cups all-purpose flour
3/4 cup sugar
2 teaspoons baking powder
1/2 cup vegetable shortening
2 eggs
1/4 cup milk
1 teaspoon vanilla extract
3 drops anise oil (optional)
3/4 cup toasted sesame seeds

TO PREPARE

1 Preheat the oven to 375° (190° C).

2 In a large bowl, sift the flour, sugar, and baking powder together.

3 Work in the shortening as you would when making pie dough, to the consistency of coarse meal.

4 Beat into the dough the eggs, milk, vanilla, and anise oil. The dough should be moist but not sticky. If the dough is too sticky, add a little more flour.

5 Take a small portion of the dough and roll out to a 1/2-inch (1.5 cm) diameter cylinder.

6 Spread some sesame seeds on a large piece of waxed paper and roll the dough in the seeds until the cylinder is completely covered.

7 Cut the dough into 1 1/2-inch (4 cm) pieces on a diagonal.

8 Place the cookies on a lightly-greased sheet pan and bake for approximately 10 to 15 minutes, or until golden brown.

9 Cool the cookies on a rack and store in an airtight container.

To serve

These cookies are also commonly served at Christmastime but are good year 'round.

Here's a very traditional Sicilian sesame seed cookie. –Damian

My grandma Carrabba made the best I ever tasted. –Johnny

They're so good that some Sicilians call them Regina or Reginetta—Queen Cookies. –Damian

Brothers Tony and Damian, Christmas morning.

Pinecone Cookies

Josephine Listi Provenzano's Pignolati

MAKES 2–3 DOZEN COOKIES

2	large eggs
1/2	tablespoon almond extract
1	cup all-purpose unbleached flour
1/4	pound (115 g) whole almonds, blanched, toasted, cut in half crosswise (see page 180)
2	tablespoons unsalted butter
2	cups granulated sugar
	Vegetable oil for frying

TO PREPARE

1   In the bowl of a small mixer fitted with a flat beater, beat the eggs and almond extract on slow speed. Add the flour a little at a time, forming a slightly sticky dough. A little more flour may be needed if the dough is too sticky.

2   Pinch off golf-ball-sized pieces of dough and roll them out on a wooden surface, working out from the center to form pencil-sized logs.

3   Place the rolled dough on a wire cooling rack or pasta drying rack and let dry for an hour, turning after 30 minutes if necessary.

4   When the dough is dry, cut each piece into a 1/4-inch (6 mm) length strip. Fry the dough in 350° (180° C) vegetable oil until golden brown.

5   Drain the dough on paper towels and let cool completely. When the dough is cool, mix with the almonds.

Pignolati are pine cones. The Neapolitans called them strufoli, in case you've ever heard of that. In the old days, these cookies were shaped like pine cones. Mrs. Provenzano is my sister-in-law's mother. –Damian

These are such little cookies, yet I think it's the hardest recipe we did on the show. –Johnny

It's tricky. And you have to make it when it's not humid. –Damian

Which means in Houston we can't make these cookies very often! –Johnny

6   Lightly butter a wooden working surface. In a large, heavy skillet, melt the sugar over medium heat.

7   Heat until the sugar becomes nice and caramel colored. It is important not to stir this mixture or it will crystallize. Add to the skillet enough of the almond-dough mixture so that the caramel just coats the almonds and dough.

8   Stir gently until the caramel is evenly distributed over the dough and the almonds.

9   Working very quickly, pour the mixture out onto the buttered surface. Using two tablespoons, grab enough hot cookie mixture to press between the two wells of the spoons, forming a small cookie.

10   Set the cookies on a sheet pan to cool, dry, and harden. Remember, you have to work fast before the caramel cools.

11   Repeat steps 6 through 10 until all the dough and almonds are used up. Store in an airtight container.

To serve

This is another Christmas cookie that is great anytime. The recipe can be a little tricky to make, but you won't be disappointed—just enjoy these cookies with a big glass of milk.

~ Cousin Salvatore Lampasas, bull riding in the Channelview Texas Rodeo, 1968.

DESSERTS

BASICS

BASICS

Stock

Beef Stock

MAKES FOUR QUARTS (3.75 L)

1	tablespoon olive oil
3	pounds (1.4 kg) beef bones
2	onions, peeled and cut into large dice
3	carrots, peeled cut into large dice
3	celery stalks, cut into large dice
2	tablespoons tomato paste
2	bay leaves
8	peppercorns
4	thyme sprigs
1	bunch parsley stems
2	cups red wine

TO PREPARE

1　Preheat the oven to 400° F (200° C).

2　Brush a cookie sheet or sheet pan with the olive oil and spread the bones on the sheet pan. Place in the oven and roast until browned, approximately one hour.

3　In a large bowl, mix the vegetables with the tomato paste to evenly coat. Set aside.

4　Remove the bones from the oven and transfer to a 6-quart (5.5 l) stockpot leaving the olive oil on the sheet pan.

5　Pour off the excess oil from the sheet pan. Place the coated vegetables on the same cookie sheet and roast for approximately 30 to 45, minutes or until lightly browned. Remove the vegetables from the oven and transfer to the stockpot.

6　With a medium-sized piece of cheesecloth, make a sachet with the bay leaves, peppercorns, thyme and parsley stems. Tie this sachet and place it in the stockpot.

7　Pour ¹/₂ cup of the red wine on the baking sheet and scrape up any bits of vegetables or bones left on the pan. Pour this into the stockpot along with the remaining wine.

8　Place the stockpot on the stove and fill it with cold water to cover the bones. Bring to a boil and then turn down to simmer. Cook for eight to twelve hours, skimming off any scum that floats to the top within the first two hours of cooking.

9　You can cook this overnight and strain it the next day through a wire mesh sieve. Discard the bones. Return the stock to the stove and reduce the volume by half.

USES: Use this stock as a base for any soup you want to add some depth and flavor to. It will keep well in the refrigerator for up to four days, or in resealable plastic bags in the freezer for up to two months.

Chicken Stock

MAKES ABOUT FOUR QUARTS (3.75 L)

4	pounds (1.8 kg) chicken bones
2	cups white wine
1	medium onion, peeled and cut into large dice
2	large carrots, peeled and cut into large dice
3	ribs celery, cut into large dice
1	fennel top, approximately 3–4 stalks
	Water to cover
2	bay leaves
8	peppercorns
1	bunch of parsley stems
5	thyme sprigs

TO PREPARE

1　Preheat the oven to 400° F (200° C).

2　Place the chicken bones on a baking sheet and roast in the oven for 35 to 45 minutes, or until dark brown. Remove the bones from the oven and place in a 6-quart (5.5 l) stockpot.

3　Add approximately 1 cup of the wine to the sheet pan and place on the stove top. With a wooden spoon, loosen the bits and pieces stuck to the pan and pour into the stockpot.

4　Roast the vegetables for about 30 minutes on the same pan until they are nicely browned. Transfer the vegetables to the stockpot and add

the remaining wine to the sheet pan and loosen the vegetable bits with a wooden spoon. Add them to the stockpot as well.

5   Next fill the pot to cover the bones and vegetables with cold water. With a medium-sized piece of cheesecloth, make a sachet with the bay leaves, peppercorns, parsley stems and thyme. Tie this sachet and place it in the stockpot.

6   Bring to a boil, then turn down to a simmer and cook for two to three hours.

7   Strain the stock through a wire mesh sieve and discard the bones. If you would like a richer stock, reduce the volume by half.

USES: This stock is great as a base for any soup or sauce. For the classic light chicken stock, omit roasting the vegetables and simply put all the ingredients into a stockpot. Cook for two to three hours and strain. Either version of this recipe will keep well in the refrigerator for up to four days, or in resealable plastic bags in the freezer for up to one month.

Fish Stock

MAKES ABOUT ONE GALLON (3.75 L)

3   pounds (1.4 kg) fish bones, preferably white fish such as halibut, snapper, sole or grouper. You can use the heads for more flavor, but make sure the gills are removed.
1   gallon cold water
2   cups white wine
3   ribs celery, coarsely chopped
1   bunch leeks, cleaned and coarsely chopped, white part only
1   small onion, peeled and coarsely chopped
2   bay leaves
8   peppercorns
1   cup parsley stems
1/4   cup thyme stems or tarragon stems, (a small handful)

TO PREPARE

1   In a large stockpot, place the bones, water, wine and vegetables.

2   With a medium-sized piece of cheesecloth,

make a sachet with the bay leaves, peppercorns, parsley stems, thyme or tarragon stems. Tie this sachet and place it in the stockpot.

3   Put on stove and bring to a boil.

4   Once the liquid is boiling, turn the heat down to simmer. With a large spoon or ladle, skim off the scum that floats to the top.

5   Cook for 30 minutes and then turn off the stove. Let this mixture sit for 15 minutes, pressing down the vegetables and bones to extract all the flavor.

6   Strain the mixture through a large piece of cheesecloth into a large bowl and place the bowl in an ice bath. (To make an ice bath, put a couple of trays of ice cubes in a large pot of water and place the bowl into the water.)

7   Stir to cool evenly. Refrigerate or freeze the stock until ready to use.

USES: You can use this stock for any fish soup recipe such as gumbo, cioppino or even chowder. If you refrigerate the mixture, it will keep for four to six days. If frozen, it will keep for up to two months.

Shrimp Stock

MAKES ABOUT ONE QUART (1 L)

     Shells from 2 pounds (900 g) medium to large shrimp
1   tablespoon olive oil
2   stalks celery, roughly chopped
1   onion, peeled and roughly chopped
4   black peppercorns
1   bunch parsley stems
1   bay leaf
2   quarts (2 l) cold water

TO PREPARE

1   Heat the olive oil in a large saucepan set on medium heat until sizzling, about two minutes. Add the shrimp shells, celery, onion, peppercorns, parsley stems and the bay leaf and cook for five minutes.

2   Add the water and bring to a boil. Turn the heat down to low and simmer for 45 minutes to

BASICS

one hour. Skim the built-up residue off the top every 10 minutes to keep the stock clear.

3   Once it's finished simmering, strain through a fine mesh strainer. Return stock to pot, turn the heat back up to high and reduce the volume by half. Cool to room temperature. It will keep for two days in the refrigerator or up to two months in resealable plastic bags in the freezer.

USES: You can use this for any seafood soups, or you can poach fish in this broth with a few of your favorite herbs.

Giblet Stock

MAKES ABOUT 3 1/2 CUPS

2	tablespoons butter
	Neck and giblets reserved from a 10–12-pound (4.2–5.4 kg) turkey
1 1/2	carrots, peeled and chopped
1	cup chopped onion
1/2	cup chopped celery
5	cups water
1	cup dry white wine
2	3-inch (8 cm) pieces of leek, white and pale green parts only
8	parsley sprigs
2	teaspoons chopped fresh thyme or 1 teaspoon dried
2	bay leaves
2	whole cloves
1/4	teaspoon whole black peppercorns

TO PREPARE

1   Melt the butter in a large heavy pot over medium-high heat. Add the neck and giblets, and sauté until brown, about 10 minutes. Using a slotted spoon, remove the neck and giblets to a plate and set aside.

2   Add the carrots, onion, celery and leek to the pot and sauté until the vegetables are brown, about 10 minutes.

3   Pour in the water and wine, and add the neck and giblets, then bring to a boil.

4   With a medium-sized piece of cheesecloth,

make a sachet with the parsley sprigs, thyme, bay leaves, cloves and peppercorns. Tie this sachet and place it in the stockpot. Reduce the heat to medium-low, partially cover, and simmer until giblets are very tender, about 1 1/2 hours.

5   Using a slotted spoon, transfer the neck and giblets to a plate. Cool. Carefully remove all the meat from the turkey neck and chop up for the gravy and/or dressing; set aside.

6   Strain the broth into a large container, pressing on the solids. Cover the chopped turkey neck and stock separately and chill. This stock can be made one day ahead.

USES: Add giblet stock to any stuffing recipe to add a richer flavor than your basic chicken stock. You can also use this in place of chicken stock in any recipe.

Breads

Cornmeal Tart Dough

MAKES ONE 11-INCH (28 CM) TART

1 1/4	cups all-purpose flour
1/3	cup fine yellow cornmeal
1	teaspoon sugar
1 1/4	teaspoons salt
6	tablespoons butter, cut into 1/2-inch (1.5 cm) cubes
3	tablespoons olive oil
1/4	cup ice water

TO PREPARE

1   In a medium bowl, mix together the flour, cornmeal, sugar and salt. Cut in the chilled butter, using the paddle attachment of a standing mixer or a pastry cutter, until the butter is evenly distributed.

2   Add the olive oil and ice water, and mix until the dough begins to come together.

3   Lightly flour your hands, then gather the dough in your hands and shape into a disk. Wrap with

plastic and chill at least one hour before using.

USES: You may use this crust recipe with any kind of savory tart, such as a quiche. It is used for our Wild Mushroom Tart (see page 14).

Rich Pie Crust

MAKES TWO 10-INCH (25 CM) PIE SHELL

2¼ cups all-purpose flour
    A pinch of salt
½ cup sugar
1¾ stick (7 ounces) (200 g) unsalted butter, cold and cubed
1 egg
1 egg yolk
1 teaspoon grated orange zest
1 teaspoon vanilla extract

TO PREPARE

1   Place the flour, salt and sugar in the bowl of a food processor fitted with a steel blade. Pulse a few times to blend. Add the cold butter and pulse five to six times, until mixture resembles a coarse meal.
2   In a small bowl, mix the egg, yolk, zest and vanilla. Add this to the food processor while it is running. Stop the mixing once ingredients are incorporated. It is important not to overmix, as the dough will be less tender.
3   Empty the dough onto a lightly-floured work surface and gently knead until it is no longer sticky. Cut the dough into two equal chunks, and pat them into flattened rounds.
4   Wrap in plastic and chill one hour.
5   After chilled, follow steps 4 through 8 in Mamma's Pie Crust recipe (see right).

USES: Use as the crust of a pie when you want the pie to be extra rich. This dough also freezes well. To freeze, place it in a pie pan after rolling. Then wrap it in a plastic bag and store in the freezer for up to three months.

Mamma's Pie Crust

MAKES TWO 9-INCH (23 CM) PIE OR TART SHELLS

3 cups all-purpose flour
1 tablespoon salt
1 cup vegetable shortening
¼ cup butter
1 egg
4–6 tablespoons ice water
1 teaspoon vinegar
    * All of the ingredients should be very cold, even the flour.

TO PREPARE

1   Sift the flour and salt together in the bowl of a food processor. Add the shortening and the butter. Pulse until the mixture has a pebble-like texture.
2   Combine the egg, 2 tablespoons of the water and the vinegar in another bowl, add to the flour, and mix until the pastry comes together. Add 2 to 4 more tablespoons of water if needed.
3   Divide into two equal balls, flatten and wrap in plastic. Chill the crust for at least 30 minutes before rolling. You don't want to overhandle the dough or it will become tough.
4   Before rolling one of the balls of dough, take it out of the refrigerator and let sit for five minutes to let it become malleable.
5   Unwrap the dough and place on a lightly-floured board, pastry cloth, or table. Gently roll out the dough with a rolling pin, starting one way then turn and roll the other. You are trying to form the dough into a circle between 11 and 12 inches (28–30 cm) in diameter. Add more flour if the dough starts to stick to the pin or board, but be careful not to add too much or the dough will become tough.
6   Once you get the dough to an 11 to 12 inch diameter, you want to carefully fold the dough in half and then in half again. This gives you a triangle shape and makes it easier to place the dough in the pie pan.
7   Place the point of the triangle at the center of a pie pan, then carefully unfold the dough to cover the entire pan.

BASICS

8   To flute or crimp the edge, place your left forefinger on the inside of the pastry rim. With the thumb and forefinger of your right hand, push the pastry from the outside, forming a V-shape groove in the dough against the left forefinger inside. Continue around the edge of the pie, forming a zigzag pattern.

USES: You are now ready to make your favorite pie recipe. This dough also freezes well. To freeze it, place in a pie pan after rolling, wrap in a plastic bag and store in the freezer for up to three months.

Homemade Breadcrumbs
MAKES FOUR TO FIVE CUPS, DEPENDING ON SIZE OF LOAF
1   loaf stale rustic Italian bread or French bread

TO PREPARE
1   Preheat oven to 175° F (79° C).
2   Take stale leftover bread and cut into cubes. Spread the stale bread cubes evenly on a sheet pan and put pan into the oven.
3   Let cook for about 45 minutes until very dry and lightly brown. Remove from the oven and let cool completely.
4   Place breadcrumbs in a food processor and grind very fine. Place breadcrumbs in a container with a tight-fitting lid. Store in the pantry.

Mamma's Bread
MAKES ONE 7–8-INCH (18–20 CM) ROUND LOAF
1 1/4 teaspoons dry yeast
    A pinch of sugar
1 1/4 cups + 1 1/2 tablespoons lukewarm water at 110° F (43° C)
3   cups unbleached all-purpose flour
2   teaspoons salt
1   teaspoon vegetable shortening
    Olive oil to grease the bowl

TO PREPARE
1   Dissolve the yeast and sugar in the 1 1/2 tablespoons of lukewarm water. After five to ten minutes you will see the yeast start to activate by bubbling and foaming. Add 1/2 cup of the remaining water.
2   Put 1 cup of the flour in a large bowl and add the yeast mixture. Start mixing and gradually incorporate the salt and shortening.
3   Add the remaining flour and, as the mixture starts to absorb the water, begin adding the remaining water until a ball of dough forms. Place the dough onto a floured board and knead for a few minutes to a nice, smooth consistency.
4   Lightly oil a large bowl. Place the dough in the bowl and cover with plastic wrap. Let the dough rise in a draft-free place for two hours, or until doubled in size.
5   Remove the dough from the bowl and knead for about four minutes. Place it on a greased sheet pan, oil the top of the dough and loosely cover with plastic wrap again. Let the dough rise a second time for another hour.
6   Preheat the oven to 450° F (230° C).
7   Gently remove the plastic wrap and, with a razor or very sharp knife, make two slashes in a crisscross shape across the top using a quick motion. Place the dough in the oven and bake for 35 to 40 minutes, or until the crust is a dark golden brown and sounds hollow when you tap it.

USES: You can eat this bread as an accompaniment to any dish, and it is great for a sandwich, such as Mamma's Oyster Loaf (see page 103).

Mamma's Breadcrumbs

MAKES ABOUT SEVEN CUPS

3   cups fine, dry Homemade Breadcrumbs (see page 170)
2   cups finely-grated Pecorino Romano cheese
6   green onions, finely chopped
1/2 cup fresh Italian parsley, finely chopped
3   cloves garlic, peeled and minced
1/3 cup finely-chopped fresh basil
1/2 tablespoon kosher salt
1/2 tablespoon freshly-ground black pepper

TO PREPARE

Place all ingredients in a mixing bowl and mix well. Store, refrigerated in an airtight container or resealable plastic bag.

USES: Perfect for most recipes calling for use of breadcrumbs.

Pizza Dough

MAKES ONE 10–12-INCH (25–30 CM) ROUND PIZZA OR
ONE 15 1/2 X 10 1/2-INCH (39 X 26 CM) RECTANGULAR PIZZA

1/2 teaspoon dry yeast
3/4 cups water at 100° F (38° C)
1   tablespoon olive oil
1   teaspoon salt
2   cups all-purpose flour

TO PREPARE

1   In a large mixing bowl, dissolve the yeast into 1/4 of the water. Let it sit for 10 minutes to dissolve. Stir in the oil and salt.

2   Add 1/2 cup of flour to start and mix thoroughly. Now start adding more water and flour, alternating and mixing well after each addition. Once you've added all the water and flour, a sticky dough should be forming.

3   Turn the dough out onto a lightly-floured surface and knead for 10 minutes. It should still be slightly sticky.

4   Place the ball of dough into a large bowl, lightly coated with olive oil. Cover with plastic wrap and let it rise for 1 to 1 1/2 hours, or until doubled in size. (You can easily double this recipe—just increase the rising time to two hours.)

5   Punch the dough down and be careful not to knead it any further as you want the dough to be relaxed and easy to work with. If you have doubled the recipe by increasing the rising time, divide the dough into two balls after you have punched it down, and freeze one of the balls.

6   If you're using a pizza stone to shape the dough, sprinkle a generous amount of flour over the surface of a pizza paddle, or alternatively you can get a 1/2-inch (1.5 cm) flexible piece of board from the hardware store and cut into about a 14 x 14-inch (35 x 35 cm) square.

7   Lightly flour a wooden work surface and place dough on work surface. Flour your hands, start from the center of the dough, and begin to shape, using a patting and stretching combination, until you achieve a 10–12-inch (25–30 cm) round (depending on how thin or thick you want it). It does not have to be perfectly round!

8   If you are using a pizza pan, brush the bottom with a little olive oil first and then start from the center of the dough, using a patting and stretching combination until you reach the edges. You may need to gently pull and stretch some parts to reach the edges.

USES: You are now ready to make your favorite pizza. The dough freezes well and is great to have on hand. Freeze one and use the other for the pizza you are making.

NOTES: To freeze the dough, wrap the ball of dough in plastic wrap and place in a freezer bag, or wrap with aluminum foil. It can be frozen for up to six months.

To thaw, place in the refrigerator overnight and then remove from the plastic bag or foil, and bring to room temperature in an oiled bowl covered with plastic wrap. When it is at the point of beginning to rise again, it is ready for making pizza according to the recipe.

BASICS

Sauces—Rubs

Tony "Nino" Mandola's Barbecue Sauce

MAKES THREE TO FOUR QUARTS (2.75–3.75 L)

5	cups Heinz ketchup
1/4	pound (115 g) butter
1	stalk celery, finely chopped
1 1/2	large yellow onions, peeled and finely chopped
1	medium green bell pepper, finely chopped
1/4	cup peeled garlic cloves, finely chopped
1	lemon, cut in half
1	bunch Italian parsley, finely chopped
3	cups water
2	tablespoons tomato paste
2/3	cup Worcestershire sauce
2	tablespoons salt
2	tablespoons freshly-ground black pepper
2	tablespoons brown sugar

OPTIONAL INGREDIENTS

1	tablespoon ground cumin
2	tablespoons chili powder
2	chipotle chilies, finely chopped

TO PREPARE

1   Place all of the ingredients in a stockpot and bring to a boil. Reduce the heat and simmer for four to five hours, uncovered, stirring occasionally.
2   Remove the lemon and squeeze its juice back into the sauce.
3   Strain the vegetables from the sauce and purée them in a blender or food processor. Return to the sauce and stir well.
4   Cool and store in an airtight container in the refrigerator.

USES: Serve with your favorite grilled chicken, ribs or even a brisket. In Texas we like to serve the sauce on the side—that way, you can add as much or as little as you like.

Cocktail Sauce

MAKES ABOUT 2 1/2 CUPS

2	cups ketchup
3	tablespoons freshly-grated horseradish or 2 tablespoons prepared horseradish
2	tablespoons Worcestershire Sauce
1	tablespoon Pick-a-Peppa Sauce
1	lemon, juiced
1	tablespoon freshly-ground black pepper
1	tablespoon Tabasco sauce

TO PREPARE

Mix all ingredients together.

USES: This sauce is great for dipping; try it on oysters, fish, or on sandwiches. You make the call!

Tartar Sauce

MAKES ABOUT 1 3/4 CUPS

1	cup mayonnaise
1/4	cup sweet pickle relish
2	tablespoons minced shallots
2	teaspoons capers
1/2	teaspoon dried tarragon
1	tablespoon Dijon mustard
2	tablespoons chopped fresh parsley
1	tablespoon freshly-squeezed lemon juice

TO PREPARE

Mix all ingredients together.

USES: This sauce is great for fish and chips, or whatever your vice may be.

Mignonette Sauce (Vinegar Dipping Sauce)

MAKES ONE CUP

1/2 cup champagne vinegar

1/2 cup sherry vinegar

1 shallot, peeled and minced

Salt to taste

1 tablespoon freshly-ground black pepper

1 teaspoon chopped fresh thyme

TO PREPARE

Mix all ingredients together in a bowl and let marinate for one to two hours.

USES: Dip a shucked oyster into the sauce or drizzle it on a bunch of shucked oysters. This can also be used as a dipping sauce for crab or shrimp.

Gorgonzola Sauce

MAKES SEVEN TO EIGHT CUPS

4 tablespoons butter

1 tablespoon peeled and chopped shallots

1/4 teaspoon peeled and chopped garlic

1 cup white wine

1 cup store-bought or homemade Chicken Stock (see page 166)

1 quart (1 l) heavy cream

1 pound (450 g) Gorgonzola cheese, cut into small pieces

TO PREPARE

1 Melt the butter in a 3-quart (2.75 l) saucepan over medium heat. Sauté the shallots and garlic until soft and translucent. Add garlic and cook a minute more.

2 Turn the heat up to medium-high, add the wine and stock, and reduce the volume by one quarter. Add the cream and heat until hot but not boiling, then add the cheese and simmer until cheese is melted.

USES: This can be served with pasta or gnocchi. Any leftover sauce can easily be frozen in one- or two-cup portions in resealable plastic bags.

Mamma's Pomodoro "Tomato Sauce"

MAKES ABOUT THREE CUPS

1/4 cup olive oil

1 medium onion, peeled and finely diced

1/4 cup garlic cloves, peeled and minced

1 28-ounce (790 g) can whole tomatoes, chopped

Salt and freshly-ground black pepper

10 large basil leaves each torn into 3–4 pieces

TO PREPARE

1 In a medium-sized stainless steel saucepan, place the olive oil, onion and garlic over medium heat and cook, stirring occasionally, for eight to ten minutes, or until onions are soft and translucent and just starting to cara-melize. Add the garlic and cool one more minute.

2 Add the chopped tomatoes and cook for 20 minutes, stirring frequently to keep the sauce from burning.

3 When the sauce is done, add the salt and pepper to taste. Add the basil leaves to the top of the sauce and cover tightly.

4 Let the sauce sit for a few minutes, then remove the lid and stir in the basil.

5 Let cool and store in the refrigerator in an airtight container.

USES: This sauce is very versatile. It can be tossed with pasta, and stewed with vegetables or your favorite fish or poultry.

BASICS

Basil Pesto

MAKES ABOUT 1¹/₂ CUPS

4   tablespoons walnuts

2   tablespoons pine nuts

¹/₂   teaspoon salt

¹/₄   teaspoon black pepper

2   whole garlic cloves, peeled

1   tablespoon softened butter

³/₄   cup firmly-packed fresh basil, leaves only

¹/₄   cup firmly-packed Italian parsley, leaves only

¹/₂   cup extra-virgin olive oil

¹/₄   cup grated Parmigiano-Reggiano cheese

¹/₄   cup grated Pecorino Roman

TO PREPARE

1   Place all of the ingredients in a blender or food processor, except the cheese and olive oil.

2   With the motor running, add the olive oil in a slow, steady stream and pulse for a few seconds, until will blended but not liquefied.

3   Remove the pesto from the food processor to a mixing bowl and stir in the cheeses.

4   Store in a glass jar or airtight container. Pesto will keep well for four to six months in the freezer and for one month in the refrigerator.

USES: You can use this pesto in salads, pasta, or even as a sauce for grilled or roasted fish.

Salsa Verde

MAKES ABOUT TWO TO THREE CUPS

1   green bell pepper, halved, cored and seeded

1   jalapeno pepper halved, cored and seeded

1   tablespoon olive oil

1   bunch cilantro, leaves only

1   cup Italian parsley, leaves only

¹/₄   cup fresh mint, leaves only

2   tablespoons minced garlic

1   tablespoon capers

10   green olives, pitted

2   tablespoons lemon juice

2   cups extra-virgin olive oil

    Kosher salt and freshly-ground black pepper

TO PREPARE

1   Preheat the oven to 500° F (260° C).

2   Brush the pepper halves with 1 tablespoon olive oil, place skin side up on a nonstick baking sheet and roast for about 15 minutes or until the skin is blackened.

3   Transfer the peppers to a large paper bag, seal and let cool for about 10 minutes. Remove from the bag and peel off the blackened skin.

4   Place the peppers along with the remaining ingredients except for the olive oil, salt and pepper in a blender.

5   Pulse the ingredients and while continuing to pulse them, slowly drizzle in the olive oil in a stream until all of the ingredients are incorporated. You may not need to use all the olive oil; it depends on the thickness you desire. Season with salt and pepper.

USES: This sauce is good on fish and chicken. We use it with our Tamale recipe and Mamma's Whole Roasted Fish recipe (see pages 85 and 100).

Johnny C's Grill Baste

MAKES ABOUT TWO CUPS

3   tablespoons butter

1   yellow onion, peeled and cut into fine dice

3   tablespoons peeled and minced garlic

2   tablespoons all-purpose flour

2   tablespoons Dijon mustard

¹/₂   cup red wine vinegar

1   tablespoon sugar

¹/₄   cup chopped fresh Italian parsley

1   lemon, juiced

TO PREPARE

1   In a saucepan, melt the butter over medium heat. Add the onions and cook until soft, about two minutes. Then add the garlic and cook an additional two minutes.

2   Add the flour and cook approximately two more minutes.

3   Then add the rest of the ingredients and stir constantly for another five minutes.
4   Remove from the heat and cool before basting the meat of your choice.

USES: Baste is great on grilled chicken. Refrigerate any extra baste in a tightly-sealed container for up to one month.

Big D's Bayou Blend

MAKES ABOUT 3/4 CUP

2   tablespoons granulated garlic
2   tablespoons onion powder
1   tablespoon dried thyme
1   tablespoon dried oregano
2   tablespoons paprika
1   tablespoon cayenne
2   tablespoons kosher salt
1   tablespoon black pepper

TO PREPARE
Place all of the ingredients in a spice grinder and pulse a few times to a powder-like consistency. Store in a dry airtight container.

Spice Rub

MAKES ONE CUP

1/2   cup brown sugar
2   tablespoons chili powder
2   tablespoons paprika
1   tablespoon black pepper
2   tablespoons salt
1   tablespoon onion powder
1   tablespoon garlic powder

TO PREPARE
Mix all ingredients together and store in an airtight container.

USES: Place the spice rub on your favorite piece of meat, fish or chicken to enhance and deepen its flavor. Let the meat marinate for at least 30 minutes. Grill or bake the items as indicated in our Barbecue Pork Spare Rib and Barbecue Beef Brisket recipes (see pages 89 and 90), or your other favorite grilling recipes. Enjoy!

Cheeses

Fresh Mozzarella

MAKES TWO POUNDS (900 G)

2   pounds (900 g) cheese curd, cut into small pieces (usually available in specialty cheese shops)
14   ounces (400 g) kosher salt
     About 4 quarts (3.75 l) of hot water 170°–180° F (77°–90° C)

TO PREPARE
1   Break the cheese curd into small pieces and place in a large bowl.
2   Add the salt to the hot water and stir to dissolve.
3   Ladle the hot water over the curd and, with two large spoons, move the curd back and forth to combine and remove the lumps.
4   Because the curd is hot, place your fingers in some ice water and then pick up a handful of the curd. Begin to stretch and work the mozzarella, trying to remove and work out all the lumps.
5   Once you've worked the mozzarella to a smooth consistency, form it into a ball. Then pinch it off into small balls about two to three inches (5–8 cm) around. Place in the ice water for a few minutes to form and cool down.
6   Remove the balls from the ice water and let them sit for 10 to 15 minutes before cutting. Store in the liquid in the refrig-erator for up to one week.

USES: Drain and slice when ready to use. Mozzarella is great in salads or on pasta and pizza.

BASICS

Ricotta Salata

MAKES ABOUT ONE POUND

1   batch of Ricotta (see below)
1–2 cups kosher salt
     Cheese molds, or plastic containers with holes punched in
     them for drainage

TO PREPARE

1   Divide the ricotta into two equal parts and
place each in plastic containers with holes
punched in for drainage. Then add the kosher salt
on top. (It should cover with up to 1/4-inch thickness of the salt.)

2   Place containers in the refrigerator with a pan
underneath for drainage. Let them stand for three
to four days, checking every few days to see that
there is still salt covering the top of the cheese.
Add more salt if needed.

3   After eight days, take the cheese out of the
containers and wash the salt off the top.

4   Invert the cheese and add more salt to the
other end of the cheese covering it again with
1/4 inch (6 mm) of salt. Every few days check to
see that there is still salt covering the top of the
cheese. Add more if needed.

5   You will know that it is done when the ricotta
is crumbly, the consistency of Feta cheese. Wash
off all the salt and pat dry. You can store this
cheese for up to two months in the refrigerator.

USES: Ricotta Salata is usually grated for either
salads or pasta.

Ricotta Cheese

MAKES ABOUT ONE POUND (450 G)

1   gallon (3.75 l) whole milk
1   quart (1 l) buttermilk

TO PREPARE

1   Combine the milk and buttermilk in a 8-quart
(7.6 l) stainless steel pot over low heat. Place a
thermometer in the liquid, without allowing it to
touch the bottom of the pan, and continue to heat
until the liquid reaches 175° F (79° C).

2   While the liquid is heating, rinse some cheesecloth and use it to line a strainer or small colander placed in a bowl.

3   When the ricotta forms on the surface of the
milk, remove it with a slotted spoon or skimmer
and place it in the lined strainer.

4   Let the ricotta drain in the cheesecloth for one
hour. Then place the lined strainer in a bowl and
place in the refrigerator to let drain for a few
more hours.

5   Store in an airtight container. Ricotta is best
when used in a few days.

USES: The fresh ricotta can be used for gnocchi,
pasta, lasagna or sauces.

Extras

Bruschetta

SERVES 8

8   slices rustic Italian bread, about 3/4-inch (2 cm) thick
     Extra-virgin olive oil
4   large garlic cloves, peeled and cut in half
     Salt and freshly-ground black pepper

TO PREPARE

1   Place bread slices on a baking sheet and toast
under a preheated broiler until the bread is lightly
toasted on both sides. In Italy the bread is placed
on the charcoal grill to give it a nice smoky flavor.

2   Remove from the oven and rub one side of the
bread with the cut side of a garlic clove. Repeat
with remaining slices of bread and garlic cloves.

3   Drizzle toast with a liberal amount of olive oil.
Season with salt and pepper.

USES: Bruschetta can be eaten like this or mounded with numerous toppings like our Cannellini Bean Purée recipe or Sun-Dried Tomato Pâté Canapés recipe (see pages 19 and 15).

White Rice

SERVES 6

2¹/2 cups long grain white rice

5   cups water or stock of your choice

1   tablespoon unsalted butter

    Kosher salt and freshly-ground black pepper

TO PREPARE

1   Add the rice to a 4-quart (3.75 ml) saucepan. Then add the butter and water or stock, and season with salt and pepper.

2   Place on the stove and bring to a boil, approximately four to five minutes. Turn down the heat to low and cook for 15 minutes, until all the liquid is absorbed.

3   Let the rice sit for three to five minutes before serving, and don't stir the rice until then, otherwise it becomes gummy.

USES: This rice is for our Cajun dishes, like Damian's Gumbo and Shrimp Étouffée (see pages 96 and 97), so it is a little stickier than usual. If you prefer less sticky rice, add a little less liquid.

Vanilla Cream Filling

MAKES 2¹/2 CUPS

2   cups milk

8   tablespoons sugar

6   tablespoons cornstarch

4   egg yolks

¹/2   teaspoon vanilla

TO PREPARE

1   Heat milk and 2 tablespoons of the sugar over medium heat until very hot but not boiling.

2   Combine the remainder of the sugar and the

cornstarch in a mixing bowl and then add egg yolks. Whisk until thick.

3   Add the hot milk, a little at a time, to the mixing bowl. Return the mixture to the stove over medium heat to thicken. When it achieves a custard consistency, remove from heat.

4   Add vanilla, mix until cool.

USES: Great for various desserts. Use rubber utensils so that cream will stay yellow.

Chocolate Icing

MAKES THREE CUPS

1¹/4 cups sugar

1   cup heavy cream

5   ounces (150 g) unsweetened chocolate

¹/2   cup unsalted butter

1   teaspoon vanilla

2   tablespoons strong coffee

TO PREPARE

1   Combine the sugar and cream in a heavy saucepan with high sides. Bring to a boil over medium-high heat, stirring constantly until the sugar has dissolved. Reduce the heat. Simmer six minutes without stirring.

2   Remove from the heat. Add the chocolate and stir to blend. Stir in the butter, vanilla and coffee.

3   Pour into a mixer bowl and chill in the freezer, stirring occasionally, until near room temperature. Remove from the freezer and beat on low speed until thickened and shiny.

USES: Excellent on cakes and used in other recipes.

NOTE: This icing freezes well. Place in a tightly-covered container. When ready to use, warm the desired quantity on the stove. Then chill in the freezer until it's thick enough to spread. Chill the balance while icing the cake so it will be even thicker to pipe rosettes, etc.

TECHNIQUES

TECHNIQUES

Peeling Garlic

1 Place the garlic head on a steady surface with the tapered end facing up at a slight angle. Hit the garlic head with the palm of your hand to separate the cloves.

2 With the flat side of a chef's knife, lightly crush the garlic clove to break the skin. Peel away the skin and cut off the root end. The garlic is now ready to slice, chop, or mince.

3 Always chop garlic as close to the time you are going to use it. Never boil, deep-fry or soak garlic in water in order to peel it—it changes the taste and removes a lot of the essential oil.

Roasting Garlic and Shallots

Garlic can be roasted in different ways, depending on how you want to use it. The whole bulb of garlic can be roasted or the bulb can be separated into individual cloves and be roasted. Shallots should be left whole.

TO ROAST GARLIC OR SHALLOTS

1 Preheat your oven to 300° F (150° C).

2 Slice the tip off both ends off the garlic or shallot. Peel away the excess paper that is around the outside of the garlic bulb. For the shallots, make sure not to remove too much of the paper.

3 Keeping the bulb whole, place in a small pan. With the garlic you could break the whole bulb into individual cloves depending on how you want to serve it.

4 Drizzle a little olive oil over the shallot or garlic head or toss with the individual cloves of garlic. Season garlic or shallots with kosher salt and freshly-ground black pepper. Cover the pan with foil or a lid and bake for 30 to 40 minutes.

5 Take out of the oven and let cool.

6 The garlic and shallot will have the consistency of a paste, that can be squeezed out and placed on bread or crackers, or used in salad dressings. You can also serve the garlic bulb whole as an accompaniment, with chicken, beef or fish, or with cheese as a first course.

Roasting Nuts

You can roast nuts either on the stove top or in the oven. Some people prefer to roast the nuts in the oven because it requires less attention. Also, you can reserve the oil from the blanched or roasted nuts and use the oil in vinaigrettes or dressing.

TO ROAST NUTS IN THE OVEN

1 Preheat oven to 325° F (170° C).

2 Place the nuts in a sauté pan or on a cookie sheet. If you plan to reserve the nut oil, add enough extra-virgin olive oil or a high-grade vegetable oil, to cover the bottom of the pan or cookie sheet.

3 Place the nuts in the oven for approximately 20 minutes.

4 For even roasting make sure to flip the nuts over.

5 If you used oil in your pan, carefully strain the nuts and reserve the oil in an airtight container for later use.

TO ROAST NUTS ON THE STOVE TOP

1 Place the nuts in a sauté pan on medium-low heat. If you want to reserve the nut oil for later use, add enough extra-virgin olive oil or a high-grade vegetable oil, to cover the bottom of the pan.

2 If you do not want to reserve any oil, place the nuts in a dry pan.

3 Toast on medium-low heat, turning the nuts with a spatula so they are evenly browned. You will need to watch them carefully using this method because the nuts tend to burn quickly.

4 The nuts should cook about 10 to 15 minutes, depending on the size of them.

5 If you added oil to the pan, carefully strain the nuts, and reserve the oil in an airtight container for later use.

Blanching and Roasting Vegetables

Blanching is a process used to peel the skin off of vegetables, keep vegetables fresh looking or speed up the cooking process, depending on what it is you wish to do with the vegetables.

TO BLANCH VEGETABLES

1 Clean and cut the vegetables into the desired shape. Keep cut vegetables similar in size to avoid overcooking or undercooking them.

2 Bring a large pot of water to a boil and add vegetables. For green vegetables, add salt to the boiling water before adding the vegetables to help keep them a brighter green.

3 Cook the vegetables al dente, between two and four minutes.

4 To avoid overcooking the vegetables and to stop the cooking process, place blanched, vegetables in a bowl of ice water. The ice water will also keep the vegetables crisp and their color bright.

TO BLANCH TOMATOES

1 Prepare the tomatoes by turning them so the stem is on the cutting board. With a sharp knife, score the skin on the bottom of each one with a small "x", making sure not to cut them too deep.

2 Place the tomatoes in boiling water and cook for eight to twelve seconds, depending on the ripeness of the tomatoes.

3 When the skin starts to peel away from the flesh, remove the tomatoes from the boiling water with a slotted spoon and place them in ice water.

4 Once they are cool enough to handle, take them out of the water and remove the skins.

5 To stuff the tomatoes, slice them into halves and scoop out the seeds and the pith.

TO BLANCH PEPPERS

Blanching peppers can be tricky and a little dangerous. Instead of being blanched in water, they are blanched in oil. This technique is used when the peppers are going to be stuffed because it cooks them to a point where they are still firm and able to hold a filling.

Blanched peppers are also used for dishes like peperonata, or they can be made into a purée.

TO BLANCH PEPPERS IN OIL

1 Fill a large pot or Dutch oven three to four inches deep with oil.

2 Heat the oil to 350° F (180° C) and place the peppers in the oil using a pair of tongs. Make sure there is no water on the peppers or it will splatter.

3 When the skin blisters, turn the peppers carefully, making sure you don't rip their skins. This will take about four to five minutes.

4 Remove the peppers from the oil, place in a bowl and cover with plastic wrap, about 10 to 15

TECHNIQUES

minutes. When cooled, the skins will slide right off.
5   At this time, you will want to carefully pull the stem out by using a sharp paring knife. Cut closely around the stem, being careful not to tear the pepper. Then with a teaspoon, scoop out the seeds and pith of each.

TO ROAST PEPPERS WITH A GAS STOVE

Roasted peppers are great used in sauces, soups and salads.

1   If you have a gas stove, take the peppers and place them directly on the flame, making sure that you don't let them fall down between the burners.
2   Char the skins to a blackened state, turning the peppers to evenly brown them.
3   Once they are completely blackened all over, place the peppers in a bowl and cover with plastic wrap for, about 10 to 15 minutes. This will let the peppers sweat and make them easier to peel.
4   When the peppers are ready, remove them from the bowl. Rub off the skin and then julienne or dice, depending on your needs.
5   You don't ever want to wash the peppers under water—this will take away the flavor you are trying to enhance.

TO ROAST PEPPERS WITH AN ELECTRIC STOVE

1   For electric stoves, you can get the same roasted effect by placing the peppers under the broiler.
2   First, cut your peppers in half and remove the seeds and stems.
3   Turn your broiler on high, place the peppers on a cookie sheet, cut-side-down, and drizzle with olive oil.
4   Place the cookie sheet in the oven about three to four inches away from the top of the oven. Cook for 15 to 18 minutes until the peppers are blistered.

5   Take out of the oven and place the peppers in a bowl and cover with plastic. Let them sweat and cool so they will be easier to peel.
6   When the peppers are ready, remove them from the bowl. Rub off the skin and then julienne or dice them, depending on your needs.
7   You don't ever want to wash the peppers under water—this will take away the flavor you are trying to enhance.

Caramelizing Onions

Caramelized onions can be used on a variety of dishes like pizza and pasta, and as an accompaniment to main courses such as meat, poultry and fish.
1   Start by trimming off both ends of each onion. Slice in half lengthwise and peel the outer skins off. Then cut the onions into thin strips lengthwise.
2   Place the onions in a sauté pan with 2 to 3 tablespoons of extra-virgin olive oil, or enough oil to make sure the onions do not stick to the pan. Place the pan on the stove over medium-high heat.
3   Once the onions begin to sizzle, turn the burner to medium-low heat, and stir every few minutes. The natural sugars will start to emerge and the onions will turn a golden brown. This process will take 15 to 25 minutes depending on the number of onions used.

Cleaning Fish and Shellfish

There are some basic things you need to know about buying and handling fish and shellfish. Most important is being able to recognize whether individual pieces are fresh.

FISH

To make sure a fish is fresh, look for the following:

1 Ocean fish should have a light smell of the sea.

2 Freshwater fish should not smell fishy at all.

3 The eyes of all fish must be bright yet dark—not white and cloudy, and not sunken.

4 The body must be firm to the touch, not soft.

5 The gills must be bright red, not brownish.

6 The skin must be smooth and still pulled tight.

TO CLEAN FISH

You can ask your fishmonger to clean the fish, or if you're feeling ambitious, you can clean it yourself.

1 To clean the fish, first de-scale it. This requires a special tool. Ask your fishmonger where you can find one. (Place the fish into a large plastic bag when you are de-scaling it to prevent the scales from flying all over the kitchen or wherever you are de-scaling it.) To de-scale the fish, start by going against the grain of the scales. Then go back and forth, rubbing evenly to take the scales off.

2 Once the scales are removed, slice the belly of the fish from under the mouth to just shy of the tail. With a small knife, cut out the stomach and all the intestines. Run the fish under cold water, rinsing out the cavity.

3 You can trim the fins, which are usually sharp, with kitchen shears.

4 If you prefer not to see the eyes of the fish on your plate, cut the head off by slicing it behind the gills with a very sharp knife. Be careful, because the bones are sometimes hard to cut through.

SHELLFISH

To make sure shellfish such as clams, mussels and oysters are fresh, look for the following:

1 Find out when the shellfish arrived in the store to make sure they have been there no longer than two days.

2 There should not be a strong odor.

3 Make sure they are alive. If they are alive the shell should be closed. If any are open, tap them on a counter. If they are alive, they should close up immediately. If they do not close up immediately, they are dead and should be discarded.

4 You can store shellfish for up to two days. To store them, cover with a moist cloth in an open container and refrigerate. After storing them and prior to preparing them, go through step 3 again to make sure the shellfish are still alive. Again, if they do not close up, throw them out.

5 Also, if shellfish do not open after cooking discard them, because they are not edible.

TO CLEAN SHELLFISH

1 To clean oysters, just run under cool water and scrub the outside of the shell with a brush. For clams and mussels, rinse them in cold water before you prepare them.

2 Then place them in a bowl of water with cornmeal. This will purge them of sand. Be sure to remove them from the water after four to five minutes. Leaving them in the water for too long will kill them.

3 When cleaning mussels, you should take the beards off, as they are tough, chewy and not really edible. With a towel, grip the beard and pull towards the base of the mussel.

TECHNIQUES

Roux Tips

Roux is a thickener that can be made in different shades; white, blonde and brown are the most common types. For our recipes, we make the darkest roux to add a nutty flavor.

To make a dark roux, add one part flour to one part oil. First heat the oil over medium heat, then gradually add the flour, stirring constantly to take out all the lumps and to keep it from burning. This will take about 15 to 20 minutes. Be very careful—if this mixture gets on your skin it will stick and burn, so be gentle while stirring. The color you are looking for is deep and dark like chocolate.

To stop the cooking process you must either take the pan off the stove and pour the roux into a sheet pan, or add diced vegetables to the roux. The second is recommended because it will cook your vegetables and stop the cooking process at the same time. But the first method is good if you want to make the roux ahead and store it for a later use. The roux can keep for up to two months in the refrigerator.

Stock Tips

When making a stock, adding roasted bones or vegetables will add more depth and flavor. This applies to any stock you wish to make, whether it is chicken, vegetable, fish, game or beef.

If you want a lighter flavor, don't brown the bones. However, we suggest when it comes to beef bones for a beef stock and vegetables for a vegetable stock you roast them for a richer flavor.

Grill vs. Barbecue

Grilling and barbecuing are often mistaken for each other but they are two very different techniques.

Grilling cooks food over a high heat to seal in the flavors. Barbecuing cooks food over a low and indirect heat, using the smoke to cook, as well as flavor, the food.

The temperature for grilling is 425° F (220° C) to over 500° F (260° C), whereas barbecuing is done between 180° F (90° C) to 250° F (130° C). When grilling, make sure the fire is not too hot or you will torch the outside of your food before the inside has had a chance to cook.

With barbecuing, make sure that your cooking vessel is pretty well sealed and then vented to optimize your cooking times. Barbecuing cooks the food slowly and, if done right, can add tons of flavor to your meat or fish. There are many different methods people swear by to make the best barbecue. Just remember that your grill needs to have varying temperatures so that you can move things around, i.e., some hot spots and some cooler spots.

[**Index**]

[Index]

[**Index**]

Acknowledgements

West 175 Productions, Inc.
President: Elizabeth Brock
Production Manager: Jamie Hammond
Associate Producer: Marla Poland

West 175 Editorial Team
Project Manager: Cassy Soden
Culinary Director: Chris Fitzgibbon
Text by: John DeMers
First Line Editors: Jennifer Steinle, Chris Rylko
Recipe Research, Development and Testing: Chris Fitzgibbon, Melissa Nyffeler

Photo Credits

Photographs by: Diane Padys, L'Image Magick, Inc.
Food Stylist: Carol Phillips   Props: Cynthia Verner
15, 36, 39, 46, 60, 66, 78, 82, 100, 102, 122, 133, 136, 148, 155, 165-167, 170-173, 175-177, 180, 181, 183

Photographs by: Watt M. Casey, Jr.
1, 3-5, 8, 9 (top right) 11, 12, 18, 20, 23, 28, 31, 35, 40, 45 (top), 47, 50, 52, 54-57, 61, 71, 73 (top), 74, 85, 92, 96, 98, 106, 115 (top), 116, 121, 124, 126, 129 (top),130, 134, 143, 146, 158, 162, 168, 169, 174, 182, 184

Set Photographs by: John Pai
25, 129, 179, 192

Archival Photographs Contributed by: The Carrabba and Mandola Families
1, 6, 9, 10, 11, 16, 24, 25 (bottom), 27, 29, 32, 44, 45 (bottom), 48, 53, 62, 72, 73 (bottom), 83, 88, 91, 108, 113-115 (bottom), 119, 128, 129 (bottom), 131, 139, 146, 153, 156, 161, 163

And this is what it all comes down to—
generous sprinklings of life, love and
oregano—for two big Sicilian boys from
Texas who love to cook and eat.

—CIAO Y'ALL!